structu
activi
issues

W9-BCN-343

CAMPUS LIFE

A SPECIAL REPORT

Campus Life

IN SEARCH OF COMMUNITY

WITH A FOREWORD BY

ERNEST L. BOYER

THE CARNEGIE FOUNDATION FOR THE
ADVANCEMENT OF TEACHING

5 IVY LANE, PRINCETON, NEW JERSEY 08540

Copyright © 1990

The Carnegie Foundation
for the Advancement of Teaching

This report is published as part of the effort by The Carnegie
Foundation for the Advancement of Teaching to explore significant
issues in education. The views expressed should not necessarily be
ascribed to individual members of the Board of Trustees of The
Carnegie Foundation.

Copyright under International Pan-American and Universal
Copyright Conventions. All rights reserved. No part of this book
may be reproduced in any form—except for brief quotations (not to
exceed 1,000 words) in a review or professional work—without
permission in writing from the publisher.

Library of Congress Cataloging-in-Publication Data

Campus life : in search of community / the Carnegie Foundation
    for the Advancement of Teaching ; with a foreword by
    Ernest L. Boyer .
        p.   cm. — (Special report)
    Includes bibliographical references.
    ISBN 0-931050-38-3
    1. College students—United States.   2. College
    environment—United States.   3. Community.
    4. Universities and colleges—United States—Administration.
    5. College presidents—United States—Attitudes.
    6. Educational surveys—United States.   I. Carnegie Foundation
    for the Advancement of Teaching.   II. Series: Special report
    (Carnegie Foundation for the Advancement of Teaching)
    LA229.C27   1990
    378. 1'98'0973—dc20   90-32888
                                                              CIP

Fifth printing, 1992

Copies are available from
CALIFORNIA/PRINCETON FULFILLMENT SERVICES
1445 Lower Ferry Road
Ewing, New Jersey 08618

TOLL FREE—U.S. Only: (800) 777-4726   FAX (800) 999-1958

PHONE: (609) 883-1759   FAX (609) 883-7413

CONTENTS

TABLES   vii

ACKNOWLEDGMENTS   ix

FOREWORD *by Ernest L. Boyer*   xi

PROLOGUE   *Search for Renewal*   1

     1.   *A Purposeful Community*   9

     2.   *An Open Community*   17

     3.   *A Just Community*   25

     4.   *A Disciplined Community*   37

     5.   *A Caring Community*   47

     6.   *A Celebrative Community*   55

EPILOGUE   *Compact for Community*   63

APPENDIX A   *National Survey of College and University Presidents, 1989*   71

APPENDIX B   *National Survey of Chief Student Affairs Officers, 1989*   101

APPENDIX C   *Technical Notes*   137

APPENDIX D   *Carnegie Classifications*   139

NOTES   141

INDEX   149

TABLES

Number	Title	Page
1	Percentage of students who study outside of class	10
2	Faculty attitudes toward undergraduate preparedness and diligence	11
3	Percentage of presidents who say harassment is a ''moderate'' to ''major'' problem on their campus	18
4	Percentage of presidents who say racial tensions and hostilities are a ''moderate'' to ''major'' problem on their campus	27
5	Percentage of presidents who rate alcohol abuse a ''moderate'' to ''major'' problem on their campus	38
6	Campus life issues of greatest concern listed most frequently by presidents	39
7	Five-year change in campus crime as perceived by student affairs officers	41
8	Percentage of presidents who say crime is a ''moderate'' to ''major'' problem on their campus	41

Number	Title	Page
9	Undergraduate attitudes toward moral issues on campus	44
10	Student affairs officers' views on the five-year change in regulation of student conduct	45
11	Percentage of presidents who rate nonparticipation by students in events a "moderate" to "major" problem on their campus	48
12	Percentage of presidents who say fraternities and sororities are a "moderate" to "major" problem on their campus	50
13	Presidents who say community can be sustained only for small groups	51
14	Percentage of presidents who report service to commuter students is a "moderate" to "major" problem on their campus	52
15	Presidents' views on the role of community	65

ACKNOWLEDGMENTS

THIS SPECIAL REPORT is the result of a year-long effort by many people. Irving Spitzberg and Virginia Thorndike, assisted by Mariann Kurtz, were the key research team, helping to organize the project from the very start. They participated in campus visits, conducted research, and drafted text. We are very grateful for their long and thorough effort.

Also conducting the site visits were Steve Diner, Martin Finkelstein, J. Eugene Haas, Gene I. Maeroff, Barbara Moran, and Jack Schuster. Their site work added vitality and immediacy to the study as well as invaluable information.

This project was in every respect a collaborative endeavor. We thank Robert H. Atwell, President of the American Council on Education, and the ACE Board of Directors, chaired by James Whalen, for suggesting this study in the first place, and for providing great encouragement and support throughout.

The American Council on Education joined with The Carnegie Foundation to conduct the survey of college and university presidents. Special recognition must be given Donna Shavlik, Blandina Cardenas Ramirez, and Russel C. Jones, and most especially to Elaine El-Khawas, who rendered invaluable editorial service. These colleagues provided rich additional information and extensive editorial comment as the manuscript was being shaped.

The National Association of Student Personnel Administrators and the Student Affairs Research, Evaluation and Testing Office of the University of Arizona joined with the American Council on Education to conduct the National Survey of Chief Student Affairs Officers. They contributed enormous energy and resources to our project, and we especially recognize the Executive Directors Elizabeth Nuss and Richard Kroc for their crucial role.

This project would not have been possible without the generous grant we received from The Henry Luce Foundation. I'm especially grateful to Robert Armstrong, Executive Director, for his great encouragement and wise counsel, which reinforced our conviction that this is a timely study.

As always I am most grateful to the staff of The Carnegie Foundation, whose work was particularly crucial to the final shape of the report. Charles Glassick, Mary Huber, and Gene Maeroff contributed immeasurably to drafting and editing the manuscript, as well as Dale Coye in the final stages. Mary Jean Whitelaw, assisted by Lois Harwood, kept track of the data and organized all of the tabular material. Hinda Greenberg and Patricia Klensch-Balmer provided invaluable support from the library. Dawn Ott and Laura Bell produced miracles of speed and quality under tight deadlines in word processing the numerous revisions, and Laura assisted with producing and proofreading the book as well. Dee Sanders not only supervised word processing, but also assisted with the design and accomplished the painstaking work of formatting and producing camera-ready pages on the desktop publisher. Jan Hempel, with great skill and under an impossibly tight deadline, edited, copyedited, and designed the book, oversaw its production, and proofread it, as well.

ERNEST L. BOYER

President
The Carnegie Foundation for the
Advancement of Teaching

X

FOREWORD

by Ernest L. Boyer

WHILE PREPARING THIS report on campus life, I've reflected frequently on the nearly four decades of higher education history I've observed firsthand. The longer I thought about it, the more I was struck by the fact that typical college-age students certainly learn outside the classroom as well as within it, and that each decade, from the fifties to the eighties, seemed to have its own distinctive flavor in relation to student life. We human beings like to slice up our lives into little segments, often defining epochs where they don't exist. But in this case the categories seem to hold.

Consider the 1950s. I was in California during this exhilarating era, and the mood was optimism unrestrained. The emphasis was on buildings, on faculty recruitment, and on the much-applauded master plan for higher education. As for students, they came in ever larger numbers, but the preoccupation at the time was focused on expansion, not the quality of campus life. Those who enrolled—even the G.I.'s—were expected to behave themselves and live by the rules. And campus regulations, though somewhat outdated, were rarely challenged.

Then came the 1960s and, almost overnight, the mood shifted from optimism to survival. The academy hunkered down as angry students folded, spindled, and mutilated computer cards, challenging the huge, impersonal enterprise higher education had become. "I'm not a number," students shouted, "I'm a person." "By what authority," they asked, "can the university arbitrarily regulate our lives?"

I recall those days with mixed emotions. There were times of anger, fear, and sadness. But I also remember those fleeting moments when the intense, yet honest, discourse with caring students revealed what a true community of learning is all about. For example, the "teach-ins," at their best, brought faculty and students out of little boxes into forums where larger, more consequential issues were considered.

Still, the 1960s will always be remembered more for the Kent State killings than for the dialogue about student life or the efforts at educational reform. Indeed, while old rules were abolished, changes were made more out of compromise than conviction, and few colleges had the imagination or the courage to replace abandoned rules with more creative views of campus life.

Perhaps the 1970s are best left unremembered. What, in fact, did happen during this uninspired decade? The good news was that higher education had survived and that serious effort was being made to open college doors to traditionally bypassed students. But in the public mind, the academy had lost its innocence, and while recovering from the onslaughts of the sixties, higher education experienced new pressures imposed by an economic downturn. Further, the baby boom was over, and college leaders heard alarming predictions that enrollments would decline and that hundreds of colleges would close.

In the 1970s, the role of students was ambiguous, at best. Faculty moved quickly to regain control over academic life, tightening general education requirements that had been reluctantly relaxed. In social matters, however, there was no comparable effort to either reestablish rules or to think about a new model of community that could replace the old. Further, the sense of urgency and altruism faded, and confronted by the harsh realities of the economic downturn, students became more concerned about credentials than confrontation.

The 1980s brought another mood to campus. The euphoria of the 1950s did not return, but neither did the anger of the 1960s, nor the depression of the 1970s. The new climate experienced by higher education was a mix of confidence and caution. Finances moderately improved, enrollments did not precipitously decline as had been predicted, faculty saw an upturn in their fortunes, and the second half of the 1980s emerged as a period of renewal.

I'm impressed that colleges and universities are focusing once again on undergraduates and on the quality of collegiate education, and today I hear more talk about the curriculum, about teaching, and about the quality of campus life than I've heard for years.

This focus on renewal is motivated, at least in part, by concerns about the darker side of student life. Confusion about governance and incidents of excessive drunkenness, incivility, and sexual and racial harassment could no longer be ignored, but more inspired motives also are involved. Everywhere, campus leaders have been asking how to make their institution a more intellectually and socially vital place. They understand that, in today's climate, new ways of imagining and creating community must be found.

The start of the new decade now presents, at least from my perspective, perhaps the most challenging moment in higher education in forty years. It affords us an unusual opportunity for American colleges and universities to return to their roots and to consider not more regulations, but the enduring values of a true learning community.

And I'm convinced that the challenge of building community reaches far beyond the campus, as well. Higher education has an important obligation not only to celebrate diversity but also to define larger, more inspired goals, and in so doing serve as a model for the nation and the world.

Search for Renewal

A MERICAN HIGHER EDUCATION is, by almost any measure, a re-markable success. In recent decades, new campuses have been built, enrollments have exploded, and today, many of our research centers are ranked world class. Still, with all of our achievements, there are tensions just below the surface and nowhere are the strains of change more apparent than in campus life.

College officials know they are no longer "parents," but they also know that their responsibilities, both legal and moral, extend far beyond the classroom, and many are now asking how to balance the claims of freedom and responsibility on the campus. At a recent meeting of college and university presidents, one participant explained his frustration this way: "We have growing racial tensions at our place. There's more crime, and I'm really frustrated about how the university should respond." Another president noted that white, black, and Asian students at his university have organized themselves into "separate worlds." "The 1990s," he said, "will be a time of confrontation."

The president of a large public university confessed: "I've been around a long time and frankly I'm more worried today than in the 1960s. Back then, you could meet with critics and confront problems head on. Today, there seems to be a lot of unspoken frustration which could explode anytime." And at the heart of these concerns was what yet another president called "the loss of community," a feeling that colleges are administratively and socially so divided that common purposes are blurred, or lost altogether.

These worries did not appear to be sentimental yearnings for a return to the days when colleges were isolated islands, tightly managed, serving the sons, and occasionally the daughters, of the

1

privileged. Today's college and university leaders understand and celebrate the dramatic transformations that have reshaped American higher education. Rather, these presidents with whom we spoke were reflecting the deep ambivalence many college leaders feel about how the campus should be governed. Every institution has clearly defined academic rules, but what about the social and civic dimensions of collegiate life? In these areas, where does the college responsibility begin and end?

It was in this context, then, that The Carnegie Foundation for the Advancement of Teaching, in cooperation with the American Council on Education, launched a study to consider social conditions on the campus. We found, first, a deep concern at most institutions about student conduct. College officials consider alcohol and drug abuse a very serious matter, one that poses both administrative and legal problems.

There is also a growing worry about crime. And while robberies and assaults have not reached the epidemic proportions recent headlines would suggest, many institutions are increasingly troubled about the safety of their students.

Especially disturbing is the breakdown of civility on campus. We were told that incidents of abusive language are occurring more frequently these days, and while efforts are being made to regulate offensive speech, such moves frequently compromise the university's commitment to free expression.

We also found that deeply rooted prejudices not only persist, but appear to be increasing. Students are separating themselves in unhealthy ways. Racial tensions have become a crisis on some campuses, and, sadly, we gained the unmistakable impression that the push for social justice that so shaped the priorities of higher education during the 1960s has dramatically diminished.

Further, even though bias against women is no longer institutionalized, sex discrimination in higher education persists in subtle and not-so-subtle forms. It shows up informally, we were told, in the classroom and occasionally in tenure and promotion decisions, too.

Finally, very early in our study, we observed an unhealthy separation between in-class and out-of-class activities. Many stu-

2

dents, we discovered, are spending little time pursuing intellectual interests beyond the classroom. The goal of many is getting a credential, and while undergraduates worry about good grades, their commitment to the academic life is often shallow. Thus, it became increasingly apparent during our study that the quality of campus life has been declining, at least in part, because the commitment to teaching and learning is diminished.

Putting it all together, we conclude that the idyllic vision so routinely portrayed in college promotional materials often masks disturbing realities of student life. On most campuses expectations regarding the personal conduct of students are ambiguous, at best. The deep social divisions that all too often divide campuses racially and ethnically undermine the integrity of higher education. Sexism continues to restrict women. The lack of commitment to serious learning among students often saps the vitality of the undergraduate experience, and we ask: If students and faculty cannot join together in common cause, if the university cannot come together in a shared vision of its central mission, how can we hope to sustain community in society at large?

These concerns about campus life are not new, but surely they reveal themselves in strikingly new ways. Consider the students. Today's undergraduates are, by every measure, more mature than the teenagers who enrolled a century or two ago. They bring sophistication and a determined independence to the campus. But we also were told that, increasingly, many students come to college with personal problems that can work against their full participation in college life. And administrators are now asking: Is it possible for colleges to intervene constructively in the lives of students whose special needs and personal lifestyles are already well-established?

Further, lots of older people now populate the campus. These nontraditional students return to college to update job-related skills or to find a new direction for their lives. Often they enroll part-time, only attend a class or two each week, and because of complicated schedules, they are unable to participate fully in campus life. Given these profound changes in the composition of today's student body,

3

administrators are now asking: Is it realistic even to talk about community in higher education when students have changed so much and when their commitments are so divided?

Diversity has also dramatically changed the culture of American higher education. America's first colleges were guided by a vision of coherence, and for the first two hundred years, college students appeared socially and economically to be very much alike. Campuses were populated mostly by men, drawn primarily from the privileged class. Virtually no black or ethnic minority students were enrolled and, at most of these colleges, a female student was "as welcome as an uninvited guest."[1]

Today, men and women students come from almost every racial and ethnic group in the country and from every other nation in the world. While colleges and universities celebrate this pluralism, the harsh truth is that, thus far, many campuses have not been particularly successful in building larger loyalties within a diverse student body, and there is disturbing evidence that deeply ingrained prejudices persist. Faculty, administrators, and students are now asking whether community can be achieved.

Consider also how the organization of higher education has been transformed. At first, the nation's colleges were small, face-to-face communities, places where the president, a few instructors, and the students all knew each other well—too well perhaps. As late as 1870, the typical American campus had, on average, only ten faculty and ninety students.[2] The president and instructors were responsible for everything involving the students.

With nineteenth century expansion, librarians were hired, then registrars. Deans became common in the 1890s and, at about the same time, vice presidents were appointed. Still, an intimate, informal atmosphere prevailed.

Colleges and universities today have become administratively complex. They are often organized into bureaucratic fiefdoms. Especially disturbing, the academic and nonacademic functions are now divided into almost wholly separate worlds, and student life concerns have become the province of a separate staff, with a dizzying array of "services" provided. The question is: How can the overall interests of students be well served in the face of such administrative fragmentation?

Most significant, perhaps, is the way campus governance has changed. Colonial colleges were, in the beginning, tightly regulated places, and the first college leaders did not doubt their responsibility to educate the whole person—body, mind, and spirit. One historian describes the climate this way: "Most members of these communities had been expected to gather permanently within their walls and to remain isolated from adult society for long periods; they were to dine together and share common lodgings in buildings sufficiently compact and secluded to permit officials to exercise a constant surveillance *in loco parentis.*"[3]

By the late nineteenth century priorities had changed. Inspired by the European university model, faculty increasingly were rewarded for research, not teaching, and professional loyalty gradually shifted from the campus to the guild. Still, college leaders did not fully free themselves from concern for the "whole person," and presidents and faculty could not escape the feeling that their responsibility went beyond the classroom. Well into the twentieth century, many colleges, both public and private, continued to require daily chapel of all students. Residence halls were still closely monitored, and women, in particular, were strictly regulated. Even when the G.I.s came to campus, colleges kept student life affairs tightly reined.

The 1960s brought historic changes. During that decade, *in loco parentis* all but disappeared. Undergraduates enjoyed almost un-limited freedom in personal and social matters, and responsibility for residence hall living was delegated far down the administrative ladder, with resident assistants on the front lines of supervision. Top admin-istrators were often out of touch with day-to-day conditions on the campus.

The problem was, however, that while colleges were no longer parents, no new theory of campus governance emerged to replace the old assumptions. Regulations could not be arbitrarily imposed—on that everyone agreed—but what was left in doubt was whether codes of conduct should be established and, if so, who should take the lead.

Unclear about what standards to maintain, many administrators sought to sidestep rather than confront the issue.

To complicate matters further, while college and university officials understood that their authority had forever changed, this shift toward a freer climate was not understood or accepted by either parents or the public. The assumption persists today that when an undergraduate ''goes off to college,'' he or she will, in some general manner, be ''cared for'' by the institution. And it's understandable that parents feel the institution has betrayed them if a son or daughter is physically or emotionally harmed while attending college.

Even state legislators and the courts are not willing to take colleges off the hook. When a crime hits the campus, as in the widely publicized drug overdose Len Bias case several years ago, the university is held responsible, at least in the court of public opinion. And many administrators now confront these urgent questions: Where does the responsibility of the college begin and end? What standards should be used to judge conduct, especially if behavior is personally and socially destructive? How can an appropriate balance be struck between the personal rights and responsibilities of students and institutional concerns?

We do not wish to suggest that colleges and universities have been unresponsive to the new realities of campus life. Indeed, our study of campus life convinced us that quite the opposite is true. We found that almost all institutions have, in recent years, expanded dramatically their student services and recruited more professional staff—counselors, financial aid officers, residence hall supervisors, and the like. Further, colleges and universities have slowly shaped new codes of conduct, often in consultation with students. Many institutions also have created imaginative new orientation programs, and have introduced workshops on social issues and all-college forums throughout the year. Student personnel administrators especially deserve high praise for their sensitive and creative work, often making decisions under difficult conditions.

Still, hardly anyone is fully satisfied with the current situation. Good work is being done to improve the quality of campus life, but student personnel professionals, who carry most of the responsibility

6

for student conduct, are expected to "keep the lid on" with no overall strategy to guide them. No one expects the campus to be problem free, and surely it's unrealistic to view the modern college as an island divorced from the outside world. But neither can colleges and universities live comfortably with a climate of endless ambiguity about how campus life decisions should be made.

How then should we proceed?

What is needed, we believe, is a larger, more integrative vision of community in higher education, one that focuses not on the length of time students spend on campus, but on the quality of the encounter, and relates not only to social activities, but to the classroom, too. The goal as we see it is to clarify both academic and civic standards, and above all, to define with some precision the enduring values that undergird a community of learning.

In response to this challenge, we propose six principles that provide an effective formula for day-to-day decision making on the campus and, taken together, define the kind of community every college and university should strive to be.

First, a college or university is an educationally *purposeful* community, a place where faculty and students share academic goals and work together to strengthen teaching and learning on the campus.

Second, a college or university is an *open* community, a place where freedom of expression is uncompromisingly protected and where civility is powerfully affirmed.

Third, a college or university is a *just* community, a place where the sacredness of the person is honored and where diversity is aggressively pursued.

Fourth, a college or university is a *disciplined* community, a place where individuals accept their obligations to the group and where well-defined governance procedures guide behavior for the common good.

7

Fifth, a college or university is a *caring* community, a place where the well-being of each member is sensitively supported and where service to others is encouraged.

Sixth, a college or university is a *celebrative* community, one in which the heritage of the institution is remembered and where rituals affirming both tradition and change are widely shared.

We recognize that these principles have to some degree informed decision making in higher education throughout the years. Our purpose in this report is to urge that they be adopted more formally as a *campus compact,* and be used more consistently as the basis for day-to-day decision making on the campus. With this in mind, we discuss in the following chapters just how the principles of community might be defined and how they might provide a new *post-in loco parentis* framework for governance in higher education, a framework that not only could strengthen the spirit of community on campus, but also provide, perhaps, a model for the nation.

8

CHAPTER 1

A Purposeful Community

F IRST, *a college or university is an educationally* purposeful *community, a place where faculty and students share academic goals and work together to strengthen teaching and learning on the campus.*

We list the principle of educational purposefulness first because it is fundamental to all others. When we began this study, our primary aim was to focus on what one president called "the social pathologies on campus," issues that had little to do, it seemed, with the academic mission. However, as we visited campuses, it soon became clear that the academic and nonacademic could not be divided. At a college or university, teaching and learning are the central functions, and if faculty and students do not join in a common intellectual quest, if they do not take the educational mission of the institution seriously, then all talk about strengthening community is simply a diversion.

It may seem unnecessary to make this point. After all, an institution of higher education is, by definition, a place for learning. But it is precisely this priority that was, we found, too often undermined. Consider the matter of how students spend their time. A recent study revealed that about half of today's full-time students are employed and that they work, on average, twenty hours every week; for part-timers, it's thirty-six hours.[1] Even more revealing, only 23 percent of today's students spend sixteen or more hours each week in out-of-class study.[2] And during campus visits, when we asked undergraduates what engaged them after class, many spoke about social life and jobs, not the academic.

9

TABLE 1

Percentage of Students Who Study Outside of Class

Per Week	1985	1988
6 or more hours	81%	70%
16 or more hours	33	23

SOURCE: Alexander W. Astin, Follow-up Trends for 1985-1988, Four Years After Entry. Unpublished data provided to The Carnegie Foundation for the Advancement of Teaching.

In an earlier Carnegie Foundation study of undergraduates, we found that about one out of every four students at four-year institutions say they spend *no* time in the library during a normal week; 65 percent use the library four hours or less.[3] Further, in a more recent survey of faculty, about two-thirds said they are teaching undergraduates basic skills they should have learned in school. Fifty-five percent believe undergraduates are "doing just enough to get by" and over half the faculty feel today's students are less willing to work hard in their studies.[4]

Several faculty members we talked with described a deficiency in the preparedness of students, especially in language skills and mathematics. One business professor told us, "I have noticed a serious decline in the ability of students to perform simple math or even arithmetic. They also seem less able to do creative thinking. In turn, the university has adjusted standards downward to accommodate these students."

A professor at a liberal arts institution said, "I do feel sorry for these young students in the 1980s, as I feel that the majority of them are grossly underprepared for coping with college-level academic study. In general, their powers of concentration are poor, their cultural literacy is poor, their scientific and technological literacy is poor, and their capacity for logical thinking, analysis, and synthesis has not been properly developed."

TABLE 2

Faculty Attitudes Toward Undergraduate
Preparedness and Diligence
(Percentage Agreeing)

	All Institutions	Research	Doctorate-Granting	Compre-hensive	Liberal Arts	Two-Year
This institution spends too much time and money teaching students what they should have learned in high school	68%	60%	64%	73%	56%	73%
Most under-graduates at my institution only do enough to get by	55	47	49	57	46	63
On the whole, undergraduates are now more willing to work hard in their studies	24	30	23	26	23	21

SOURCE: The Carnegie Foundation for the Advancement of Teaching, *The Condition of the Professoriate, Attitudes and Trends, 1989* (Princeton, NJ: Carnegie Foundation for the Advancement of Teaching, 1989), pp. 20-22.

In addition to complaints about student preparation, faculty say that students are not always willing to work hard in college. One professor at a doctorate-granting institution said, "A large percentage of students today seem to want to succeed (in school, in life) without making a substantial effort to really comprehend. As unlikely as it may seem, students frequently *say* that some subordinate will do their detail/analysis work for them, therefore, they do not have to understand."

These generalizations don't apply, of course, to all institutions. Many are successful academically and others are brilliantly succeeding. Further, no one expects undergraduates to be round-the-clock academic grinds. Students need open spaces, moments alone, occasions to relax with friends. Still, as the first priority, a college should be committed to excellence in education, and college, at its best, is a place where students, through creative teaching, are intellectually engaged.

But there is another side to the equation. Faculty, because of the reward system, are often not able to spend time with students, especially undergraduates. We found that, on too many campuses, teaching frequently is not well rewarded, and especially for young professors seeking tenure, it's much safer to present a paper at a national convention than it is to spend time with undergraduates back home.

And yet at a college or university of quality, the classroom should be the place where community begins. Educator Parker Palmer strikes precisely the right note when he says, "Knowing and learning are communal acts."[5] If we view student life from *this* perspective, then strengthening community rests not just with counselors, chaplains, residence hall supervisors, or the deans, but also with faculty who care about students and engage them in active learning.

With this vision, the great teachers not only transmit information, but also create the common ground of intellectual commitment. They stimulate active, not passive, learning in the classroom, encourage students to be creative, not conforming, and inspire them to go on learning long after college days are over. We urge, therefore, that colleges and universities reward not only research and publication, but great teaching, too.

Faculty may sometimes find the lecture format appropriate, but small seminars are also needed so that undergraduates can have more direct access to professors in a setting where dialogues thrive and relationships grow, not just between teachers and students, but among the students themselves. In the classroom, students should learn to cooperate, not just compete, and we recommend, therefore, that all lower-division students have at least one course each semester with an enrollment of no more than thirty students each. Further, we urge that all students work together occasionally on group assignments, within

12

large lecture sections, to underscore the point that cooperation in the classroom is as essential as competition.

Beyond the classroom, community can be strengthened by academic departments that bring students and faculty together. The department is, perhaps, the most familiar, most widely accepted organizational unit on campus. As students select a major, they join with faculty to pursue common academic interests and often forge social loyalties, too. In addition to their advising role, departments can become a creative intellectual and social unit on the campus through special seminars, lectures, and social events for students and faculty. Many academic departments already do these things, and we urge that the commitment to make the department a powerful unit of community be broadened.

All college events—those that cut across departmental interests—can be especially valuable in stirring a common intellectual purpose on the campus. Ohio Wesleyan University, for example, selects a theme each year to be studied by everyone on campus for an entire term. In the fall of 1989, the theme was "The Impact of Technology on Culture." Every Wednesday at noon, visiting speakers addressed such topics as "Technology's Impact on the Amish" and "Weaponry Over the Years." Also there were days when everyone came together in all-college seminars and forums. The entire campus became a classroom.

The Red Barn, located on the edge of the University of Louisville, has, for twenty years, sponsored arts and educational programs that bring together students, faculty, staff, and Louisville residents of all ages. On the campus of the University of California, Berkeley, students hold forth almost daily from the steps of Sproul Hall. At Earlham College in Indiana, tables in the dining hall often are covered with hand-outs on social issues, and the Opinion Board in the Earlham Student Union is another forum for vigorous exchange. Weber State College in Utah, a campus where most students commute, has set aside one morning every week for a wide range of student activities, and for a campuswide convocation.

Residence halls can be classrooms, too. At the University of Vermont, a Living-Learning Center—a kind of college-within-a-

13

college—houses more than five hundred students who work together. The Center has faculty apartments, classrooms, and its own dining room; students go on field trips and attend special seminars in addition to their regular academic work. Indiana University has sections set aside in some residence halls where faculty meet with students. Several years ago the University of Miami renovated residence halls so senior faculty and administration could "live in." Examples such as these can be found on campuses from coast to coast.

Ideally, a commitment to learning—a shared sense of intellectual excitement—pervades the entire campus. Lectures, informal debates, singing groups, orchestras and bands, theater productions, dance concerts, the student radio and newspaper, literary journals, film societies, debate clubs—all richly promote a community of learning through an "out-of-class curriculum" where the intellectual, aesthetic, and social dimensions of campus life thrive. In such a climate the purposefulness of the college or university is apparent everywhere.

Finally, a discussion of the intellectual life of a community of learning must focus on the curriculum itself. The course of study a college offers provides students an academic road map, and a shared intellectual discourse can be achieved most successfully, perhaps, through a well-planned general education sequence, a core curriculum with coherence.

The sad truth is, however, that at far too many institutions the "distribution requirements" of general education are unfocused. They encourage randomness, not coherence, and create the strong impression that the college has no larger sense of purpose. At one institution in our study, students and faculty compared the curriculum to a fast food restaurant. "We're kind of like a McUniversity," one student told us. "A smorgasbord of fast food."

We conclude that if the spirit of community is to be renewed—if the intellectual life is to be central—the curriculum must illuminate larger, more integrative ends. A coherent general education sequence should introduce all students, not only to the essential fields of knowledge, but also to connections across the disciplines, and help them apply knowledge to their own lives.

14

We are encouraged that, in recent years, colleges and universities all across the country are, in fact, redesigning general education to achieve these essential aims. At Brooklyn College, the core curriculum consists of ten areas that every student, regardless of major, must study. These include: mathematical reasoning; sciences; art and music; philosophy; western culture; the study of power and social organization in America; European and American history; landmarks of literature; third world cultures; and a foreign language. This cluster provides a solid grounding in academic inquiry and also becomes a base of common learning for all students.

Bethany College in West Virginia has a perspectives program that organizes general education into eight categories: aesthetic judgment, experimental science, global awareness, historical foundations, human personality and behavior, Judaeo-Christian tradition, quantitative reasoning, and social institutions. This core curriculum also introduces students to the disciplines, while relating liberal arts education to the working world and to consequential issues in students' lives.

Saint Anselm College in Indiana has a cluster of courses built on the theme "Portraits of Human Greatness." Two freshmen core courses cover the many ways "human greatness" has been described from ancient to modern times. One recent unit included a study of the warrior, the prophet, the philosopher, the lawgiver, the disciple, the knight, the townsman, and the medieval scholar. Another unit used Dante's *Divine Comedy* to inquire about God and humanity. Two other courses focused on the lives of noteworthy individuals—Michelangelo, Martin Luther, Queen Elizabeth I, Cervantes, Pascal, Thomas Jefferson, Beethoven, Darwin, Lenin, Gandhi, Sartre, and Pope John XXIII.

Recently, the State University of New York at Buffalo proposed a new general education curriculum for arts and science students. The plan begins with a foundation course in language and writing skills. There are "common experience" courses in world civilization, American pluralism and the search for equality, scientific inquiry, great discoveries in science, mathematical science, physical or biological science, literature and the arts, and social and behavioral sciences. All students in their fourth year also would complete an "integrative course," thus running general education vertically from the freshman to the senior year. These are only a few examples of curricular changes in a national push to revitalize the core of common learning.

We conclude that the quality of a college or university must be measured first by the commitment of its members to the *educational* mission of the institution. It is in the classroom where community begins, but learning also reaches out to departments, to residential halls, to the campus commons. The curriculum, too, if properly designed, should intellectually integrate the campus. In a *purposeful* community, learning is pervasive.

CHAPTER 2

An Open Community

SECOND, *a college or university is an* open *community, a place where freedom of expression is uncompromisingly protected and where civility is powerfully affirmed.*

The educational mission of higher learning is carried on through reasoned discourse. The free expression of ideas in a community of learning is essential, and integrity in the use of symbols, both written and oral, must be continuously affirmed if both scholarship and civility are to flourish. The quality of a college, therefore, must be measured by the quality of communication on campus.

Proficiency in language means, first, the ability to read with comprehension, write with clarity, and effectively speak and listen. This is the minimum. But if a higher learning institution is to fulfill a larger function—if it is to sustain a climate of reasoned discourse—the quality of communication on campus must be measured not just by *clarity* of expression, but by *civility* as well.

That's the goal, to be assured that students speak and listen carefully to each other. But during our study, we were troubled to discover that, on too many campuses, incivility is a problem and, all too frequently, words are used, not as the key to understanding, but as weapons of assault. Especially disturbing is the fact that abusive language is revealed most strikingly in racial, ethnic, and sexual slurs.

Offensive language can crop up almost anywhere, but the problem appears to be most acute at large research and doctorate institutions, where more than 60 percent of the presidents we surveyed said "sexual harassment" is a problem, and where half also listed "racial intimidation and harassment." Further, when presidents were asked how they would improve campus life, 86 percent of those at large

17

TABLE 3

Percentage of Presidents Who Say Harassment Is a "Moderate" to "Major" Problem on Their Campus

	All Institutions	Research & Doctorate-Granting	Compre-hensive	Liberal Arts	Two-Year
Sexual harassment	28%	62%	32%	30%	20%
Racial intimidation/harassment	16	48	18	15	13

SOURCE: The Carnegie Foundation for the Advancement of Teaching and the American Council on Education, National Survey of College and University Presidents, 1989.

universities said there should be "new and revised statements on civility and respect for others."[1]

Outside speakers often pose a special problem. At a large state university, the black student union invited Louis Farrakhan to speak. Some students and state legislators opposed the use of student fees to pay a speaker they considered a "black racist," and objected to using state money to provide security. The university defended the students' right to invite any speaker, regardless of his views, and also declared that the threat of disruption should not abridge free speech. The event occurred without serious incident.

At another place the drama department invited a black actress to perform a one-woman show called "Nigger Cafe." The dean who approved the performance felt it would help students better understand racial issues. The invitation was opposed, however, by a senior black faculty member and members of the black student union, who found the title offensive. Pressure against the performance became so great that the dean withdrew the invitation.

Elsewhere, students erected a shantytown to express their displeasure with the trustees' stand on South African investment. The shanties, standing at the very heart of the campus, made a powerful visual statement, dividing the college down the middle. Opposing students tore the buildings down. The president said this abridged free expression and the next morning helped rebuild the shanties.

No one wants to be cast in the role of censor. Still, civility and courtesy lie at the very heart of academic life, and many college and university presidents are urgently looking for ways to define the boundaries of acceptable speech. Academic leaders have both an educational and moral obligation to be concerned about abusive language, and 60 percent of the chief student affairs officers we surveyed report that their campus now has a written policy on bigotry, racial harassment or intimidation. Another 11 percent say they are working on one.[2]

But colleges are finding it difficult to balance free speech with constraint. Several years ago, Tufts University sought to prohibit verbal and written expression that could be viewed as harassment. This move was sparked by the appearance on campus of a T-shirt imprinted with a message judged by many to be demeaning to women. Under the new rule, a student could not wear the offensive shirt in a public space. Students, in demonstrating against the rule, divided the campus with chalk lines—into restricted and free speech zones. The policy was withdrawn.

Several years ago, the University of Michigan adopted guidelines that defined appropriate speech standards in various campus settings—public, educational, and residential. The policy seemed carefully crafted, but subsequent cases reveal, once again, just how hard it is to establish boundaries.

- In a classroom, a student stated his belief that homosexuality is a disease, and said he intended to develop a counseling plan for helping gays become straight. A classmate filed a charge of sexual harassment. A hearing panel unanimously found that the student had, indeed, violated the university's policy—but he was not convicted. A court later found that the student should not have had to endure the process in the first place, since his remark was a part of a legitimate classroom discussion.

19

- A white student in a pre-dentistry course stated that he had heard that minorities had a difficult time in the course and were not treated fairly. The minority professor who taught the class filed a complaint, believing the comment was unfair and hurt her chances for tenure. The student was then counseled about the policy and wrote a letter apologizing for his comments.

The Court, in reviewing these incidents, ruled that the university policy violated the First Amendment rights of free speech. Specifically, the judge wrote: ''It is clear that the policy was overbroad both on its face and as applied. . . .'' He concluded that ''it is an unfortunate fact of our constitutional system that the ideals of freedom and equality are often in conflict. The difficult and sometimes painful task of our political and legal institutions is to mediate the appropriate balance between these two competing values.''[3]

Given conflicting signals, how should colleges proceed? Is it possible to protect freedom of speech and also keep abusive language from poisoning the campus? Since the 1960s, it has been widely accepted law and practice that campuses can regulate the time, place, and manner of speech. They cannot, however, regulate content without violating the spirit of inquiry upon which both scholarship and a free society depend. Indeed, the necessity of assuring free expression on campus derives not only from values rooted in the United States Constitution, but also from the very nature of the university itself.

We conclude that restrictive codes, for practical as well as legal reasons, do not provide a satisfactory response to offensive language. Such codes may be expedient, even grounded in conviction, but the university cannot submit the two cherished ideals of freedom and equality to the legal system and expect both to be returned intact. What the university *can* and *should* do, we believe, is define high standards of civility and condemn, in the strongest possible terms, any violation of such standards.

Perhaps the most enduring policy statement on freedom of expression has been the 1975 report of a Yale University committee, chaired by Professor C. Vann Woodward, and incorporated into the Yale Undergraduate Regulations. The committee wrote:

> No member of the community with a decent respect for others should use, or encourage others to use, slurs and epithets intended to discredit another's race, ethnic group, religion, or sex. It may sometimes be necessary in a university for civility and mutual respect to be superseded by the need to guarantee free expression. The values superseded are nevertheless important and every member of the university community should consider them in exercising the fundamental right to free expression. . . . The conclusions we draw, then, are these: even when some members of the university community fail to meet their social and ethical responsibilities, the paramount obligation of the university is to protect their right to free expression. . . . If the university's overriding commitment to free expression is to be sustained, secondary social and ethical responsibilities must be left to the informal processes of suasion, example, and argument.[4]

Above all, campus leaders must not only protect freedom of expression, but also affirm civility by the force of their own example. Stephen B. Sample, president of the State University of New York at Buffalo, made the point powerfully in a call he made to the entire university community to speak out against intolerance. President Sample put it this way:

> As long as we let those small moments pass without calling attention to the injustice they represent, the threat to justice everywhere will continue. Thus, I call upon all of us to remember our responsibilities to ourselves and each other by speaking out against bigotry and intolerance whenever and wherever they occur. Only by this vigilance in our daily lives can we help make justice everywhere possible.[5]

21

Derek Bok, president of Harvard University, in response to a grossly demeaning letter about women circulated by a student club, argued that such communication, while offensive, should not be suppressed:

> Although such statements are deplorable, they are presumed to be protected under the Constitution and should be equally so on the campus as well. Why? The critical question is: Whom will we trust to censor communications and decide which ones are "too offensive" or "too inflammatory" or too devoid of intellectual content? . . . As a former president of the University of California once said: "The University is not engaged in making ideas safe for students. It is engaged in making students safe for ideas."[6]

President Bok then issued a strong and public denunciation of the letter and its authors:

> The wording of the letter was so extreme and derogatory to women that I wanted to communicate my disapproval publicly, if only to make sure that no one could gain the false impression that the Harvard administration harbored any sympathy or complacency toward the tone and substance of the letter. Such action does not infringe on free speech. Indeed, statements of disagreement are part and parcel of the open debate that freedom of speech is meant to encourage; the right to condemn a point of view is as protected as the right to express it.[7]

We cannot leave our inquiry into the uses of language without pointing to a higher standard. During campus visits we were troubled that debates about the limits of expression were often argued in administrative, even legalistic terms. Rarely was attention given to the fact that careless words can be deeply wounding. Words were being analyzed with insufficient care being given to the painful feelings they evoked.

We believe that standards of communication, especially on a college campus, must go far beyond correct grammar or syntax; they even must extend beyond the "civility" of the message being sent. A higher standard is to view communication as a sacred trust. The goal of human discourse must be to both speak and listen with great care and seek understanding at the deepest level, and this expectation takes on special significance as the nation's campuses become increasingly diverse.

Many students, because of their own cultural isolation, bring prejudices to campus that serve to filter out the feelings of people from racial, ethnic, and religious backgrounds different than their own. But if communication does not go beyond the formality of the words and yield a deeper understanding of who people really *are,* prejudice persists. Wayne Booth of the University of Chicago captured this high standard when he wrote: "All too often our efforts to speak and listen seem to be a vicious spiral moving downward. But we have all experienced moments when the spiral moved upward, when one party's efforts to listen and speak just a little bit better, produced a similar response, making it possible to move on up the spiral to moments of genuine understanding."[8]

In an *open* community, freedom of expression must be uncompromisingly defended. Offensive language must be vigorously denounced. But in the end, good communication means listening carefully, as well, and achieving moments of genuine understanding. "No law can mandate that everyone adore everyone else," as President Sample notes, "but especially in the university community we *can* expect everyone to respect the rights and dignity of everyone else. Indeed, we must demand it."[9]

CHAPTER 3

A Just Community

THIRD, *a college or university is a* just *community, a place where the sacredness of each person is honored and where diversity is aggressively pursued.*

Higher learning builds community out of the rich resources of its members. It rejects prejudicial judgments, celebrates diversity, and seeks to serve the full range of citizens in our society effectively. In strengthening campus life, colleges and universities must commit themselves to building a *just* community, one that is both equitable and fair.

For almost two centuries colleges were, with few exceptions, a haven for the privileged. They catered to the most advantaged, enrolling young men who, upon graduation, were often placed in still higher positions of privilege and power. Slowly the admission doors swung wider and more women and minority students came to campus, and during the 1960s, the nation's colleges and universities, in response to the eloquent call for simple justice, pushed aggressively to broaden opportunities for historically by-passed students.

Sadly, this sense of urgency has, in recent years, diminished and the nation's colleges and universities have largely failed to provide sustained leadership in the drive for equality of opportunity in the nation. Rather than push vigorously their own affirmative action programs, aggressively recruiting minority students into higher education, they turned to other matters, and a historically important opportunity to advance the cause of human justice was forever lost.

America and the nation's campuses are, once again, afflicted by a deepening polarization along racial and ethnic lines as young blacks and Hispanics remain socially isolated and economically deprived. Recently the American Council on Education reported that the number of low-income, black high school graduates going on to college actually *dropped* from 40 percent in 1976, to 30 percent in 1988; for low-income Hispanics, the college participation rate fell from 50 percent in 1976, to 35 percent in 1988.[1] This represents an educational failure of intolerable proportions.

We strongly recommend that, during the decade of the nineties, every college and university reaffirm its commitment to equality of opportunity, establish goals for minority enrollment, and select precise timetables, too. This means working closely with the schools, and we propose that colleges begin recruiting black and Hispanic students when they're still in junior high.

But the issue is more than access; it has to do with the lack of support minority students feel once they have enrolled, and there are alarming signals that racial and ethnic divisions are deepening on the nation's campuses. College and university presidents told us that suspicions are intense, and the black student body president at the University of Massachusetts, Amherst, expressed herself this way: ''I think within the next decade we will see an increase in racial altercations, not just white on black, but black on white.''[2]

In our administrative survey, one in four of all college and university presidents reported that racial tensions are a problem on campus. And the issue is especially troublesome at large universities, where more than two-thirds of the presidents at research and doctorate institutions said ''racial tensions and hostilities'' are a problem. When asked their views for improving campus life, presidents at these institutions said ''greater racial understanding'' was a priority.[3]

Many administrators and faculty can recall the 1950s when Rosa Parks boarded a bus and made history with her decision to take a seat up front. They remember the sixties when black students sat at a lunch counter and defied centuries of prejudice with a simple request for service. They recall the decade when United States Marshals had to escort James Meredith onto the campus of ''Ole Miss.'' This was the

TABLE 4

Percentage of Presidents Who Say Racial Tensions
and Hostilities Are a "Moderate" to "Major"
Problem on Their Campus

All Institutions	Research & Doctorate-Granting	Comprehensive	Liberal Arts	Two-Year
24%	68%	20%	28%	15%

SOURCE: The Carnegie Foundation for the Advancement of Teaching and the American Council on Education, National Survey of College and University Presidents, 1989.

decade when Martin Luther King, Jr., led a great crusade to affirm the dignity of all.

College leaders may recall these historic times, but many students do not, and today some reject, even resent, the idea of inclusion. "We carry a stigma," said one Chicano student. ". . . When I first came here as a freshman, a white undergraduate said to me, 'You're here but my friend, who is better qualified, is not.'"[4] At a research university in the Southwest, an assistant dean of students commented: "Most white students don't understand why white applicants are being left out. Black students are asked, 'Did you get in here because you are black?'"

Prejudice was reported elsewhere. During one of our campus visits, the black homecoming queen said there was graffiti in the women's restroom attacking her. At another place, a black candidate for a student government position said a white student he had asked to vote for him responded: "Is the other candidate on your ticket a nigger too?" A Mexican-American student at a southern university was quoted in *Change* magazine as saying: "People will joke around—at least I hope they are joking—and say, 'Oh, he's Mexican, hide your wallet.' Or, 'Do you have a switchblade?'"[5]

At Stanford University several years ago, two white freshmen and a black sophomore had a debate about the influence of blacks on music. As part of the conversation, the black student said that Beethoven was a mulatto. The white students were skeptical and later, after a drinking bout, put a poster outside the black student's room depicting Beethoven as a stereotyped black. Although the white students described their intent as parody, the black student and his friends interpreted the act as racist, leading to a major confrontation.[6]

Virulent forms of anti-Semitism are flairing up as well. A recent front-page article in *The Chronicle of Higher Education* said that Jewish students and faculty members are reporting more anti-Semitic acts on their campuses than at any other time in the past ten years. Among the offensive acts described were the appearance of catalogs promoting neo-Nazi literature, the painting of swastikas on a Hillel building, and the mocking of Jews as the *theme* of a fraternity party.[7]

Incidents such as these speak volumes about the hostile climate many minorities feel on campus. Professor Patricia Williams, the first black woman to teach at Stanford's school of law, described in moving language the deep, personal hurt, as well as insult, such encounters can elicit:

> The most deeply offending part of the injury of the Beethoven defacement is its message that if I ever manage to create something as significant, as monumental, and as important as Beethoven's music, or the literature of the mulatto Alexandre Dumas or the mulatto Aleksandr Pushkin's literature—if I am that great in genius, and perfect in ability—then the best reward to which I can aspire, and the most cherishing gesture with which my recognition will be preserved, is that I will be remembered as white . . . The issue is about the ability of black and brown and red and yellow people to name their rightful contributions to the universe of music or any other field. It is the right to claim that we are, after all, part of Western Civilization. It is the right to claim our existence.[8]

28

Throughout higher education we found that Hispanic, Jewish, Polish, Italian, Muslim, Arab, Vietnamese, and Haitian student associations have organized themselves in their own separate groups—and on at least one campus a white student union has been formed. Organizations that celebrate diversity have an important role to play, but exclusive groups can generate conflict.

Black student organizations seem to stir the most misunderstandings, even heated controversy, on campuses. And yet those criticizing blacks for being "separatist" were themselves often grouped together, in less obvious ways, so that black students were effectively being held to a double standard. At a small liberal arts college in the East, a white student suggested that the mere existence of a black student union "polarized the students." A black student at an elite private university agreed with this position. He told one of our researchers: "I get a lot of flack because I don't belong to the black student union. I think it's stupid to have a Drama Association and a Black Drama Association" on this campus.

On the other hand, an officer of the student union responded aggressively to the charge that blacks were "separatists." "If black students were inclined toward separation," he insisted, "they never would have come to this predominantly white institution in the first place. The problem is that blacks, once they come to this campus, discover that they need support from fellow blacks to emotionally survive."

This student then told us his experience. "Soon after I got here I found out that I was one of only twelve black people in the freshman class. I did not expect that to be a problem. I was wrong. As the semester progressed, I realized that many whites on campus were not making the same effort to continue relationships that I was. I then realized that the 'black separatists' were the only people who took me at face value and at the same time were themselves with me. I still have white friends, but they are the exceptions who take me for what I am. Basically, we 'black separatists' have set ourselves apart, on one level, because we were forced to do so."

Here's how another student expressed his concern: "Minority students tend to all come together, because they are so small in number and black students just don't feel welcome. Everything is separate for us. We have a totally different idea of what a party is. We don't get together with whites. It's kind of hard when you don't see anyone who can really understand you.''

Striking a balance between special groups and the larger community is, we found, one of the most difficult challenges administrators now confront. The president of one elite university described his concern to us this way:

> The question which intrigues me is the role of any homogeneous subset of students who wish through some exclusive arrangement to spend some of their time together. This could be groups of women or men or blacks or athletes. The key point is that membership in these groups is selective and exclusive. My own observation is that as diversity on our campuses increases, many students feel an increasing desire to participate in some homogeneous group.
>
> Last week I asked a student what her main disappointment and her best experience on campus had been. Her chief complaint was the lack of sufficient diversity, but her best experience was her participation in an all-female social club!
>
> Almost every month I'm asked by an exclusively black organization to give them official recognition. Their claim is usually that these organizations give them strength to participate in the larger community. I'm trying to understand how a university that's committed to diversity can have official interactions with organizations that are avowedly *exclusive,* even if they have desirable ends.

It's understandable that students, especially those who feel vulnerable, want to meet together. Indeed, self-generated activity by student groups bring vitality to the campus. Frequently they are the most effective means of creating a fundamental sense of belonging, and through them students gain a feeling of belonging to the larger campus community. But we're also impressed by the tensions created as subgroups organize themselves along racial, ethnic, or gender lines. And we worry about the racial tensions on the campus, the lack of trust, the singular lack of success many colleges and universities have had in creating a climate in which minority students feel fully accepted on the campus.

There is no easy answer. On the one hand, we believe students should join together, as they have always done, to pursue special interests. Minority students especially have a need to organize themselves for support in an environment that is often perceived to be insensitive, even hostile. But we also urge that student groups reach out, authentically, to one another. They should try to explain their own purposes and understand the purposes of others and meet, if possible, as individuals, one on one.

For example, would the student leaders of campus organizations be willing to spend time together, in a summer retreat, in search of common ground? Could we expect that all subgroups also would affirm the larger purposes of the institution? And could the six principles set forth in this report provide a framework by which the legitimacy of every campus group might be judged?

We also suggest that every college and university conduct a detailed study of the racial climate on its campus, to learn more about itself. The goal of such an inventory would be to gather more precise information about the depth of ethnic and racial tensions, to better understand how students from various groups really feel about their situation, how administrative officers and academic groups are viewed, and to hear how various minority students feel the climate might be improved. This information should be shared in an organized way with the campus community at every level—students, faculty, and administrators.

The president at Wellesley College, several years ago, named a Task Force on Racism to study the experiences of racial minorities at that institution and make recommendations for change. The Task Force not only probed academic and nonacademic activities, but also inquired into the sensitivity of administrative officers. The results revealed how various student groups can view the same campus in strikingly different ways.

Upon receiving the report, the president made the following declaration. "It is important that we confront racism, recognizing its complexities and its deep-rootedness in our culture. We must face up to its particular manifestations at Wellesley, not treat it gingerly and pretend it's irrelevant to us."[9] As poet Adrienne Rich has said so well in *Lies, Secrets, and Silence:*

> I believe the word *racism* must be seized; grasped in our bare hands, ripped up out of the sterile or defensive consciousness in which it so often grows, and transplanted so that it can yield new insights for our lives. . . . I am convinced that we must go on using that sharp, sibilant word, not to paralyze ourselves and each other with repetitious, stagnant doses of guilt, but to break it down into its elements. . . . Our stake . . . in making these connections, is not abstract justice; it is integrity and survival.[10]

Above all, colleges and universities should seek to build racial and cultural understanding, not just socially, but *educationally* as well. Students should take time in their formal program of instruction to learn about the heritage and traditions of other racial and ethnic groups, so that social relationships can be put in context. The University of Minnesota requires that all students take at least two courses on different American cultures. Mt. Holyoke and Tufts University have a similar requirement. The University of California, Berkeley, Faculty Senate recently ruled that all undergraduates take at least one course in American Cultures. This broader view of the curriculum is necessary, we believe, for every higher learning institution.

Affirming diversity touches the community in other ways as well. It was not until the late 1960s that women in significant numbers

32

entered higher learning institutions and pursued fields of study traditionally reserved for males. Prospects for the professional advancement of women also improved and funds for women's studies programs became available. Today, according to recent studies, freshmen women have higher intellectual and social self-confidence. Their degree aspirations and career choices in such fields as business, law, medicine, dentistry, and computer programming are quite similar to those of men.[11]

Still, it was regularly apparent during our study that sexist attitudes persist. An adult student at a community college in the Southwest recalled: "My professor told me I should not be an engineer because I am Hispanic and a woman. I went home and cried. Then, I decided not to complain. I'd get my degree and show him." A younger undergraduate in an elite university in the Northeast said: "My professor told me not to bother to apply to business school because they never take women." At this same institution, another woman reported that when she registered for an upper-level calculus course the male instructor said: "This is an advanced course. Why are you taking it?"

Men still seem to talk most often in class, and women students, who are often overshadowed, may submit excellent written work, yet wait until after class to approach a teacher privately about issues raised in the discussion. Not only do men talk more, but what they say often appears to carry more weight with some professors, and this pattern of classroom leaders and followers is set very early in the term.[12]

More blatant acts of prejudice are frequently reported. In a 1983 study, 40 percent of undergraduate women reported experiencing sexual harassment[13] and a Harvard University survey found that 34 percent of women undergraduates at that institution reported harassment from a person in authority.[14] At a small eastern university in our study, a sophomore reported that members of the women's caucus "get insults shouted at them." And at a southern research university, the managing editor of the newspaper complained about T-shirts reading "Ten reasons why beer is better than women." At yet another campus, a female student who worked part-time with the maintenance crew complained of lewd remarks.

Defining sexual harassment is a critical step toward its elimination, and we recommend that every college and university codify its own policy and consider sexual harassment as it affects the full range of campus life. Princeton University has a policy that is implemented through education, confidential counseling, procedures for lodging formal complaints, and remedies ranging from mediation to disciplinary action. The Princeton code, which is similar to that of other campuses, defines sexual harassment as:

> unwelcome sexual advances, requests for sexual favors, and other verbal or physical conduct of a sexual nature when submission to or rejection of such conduct is made implicitly or explicitly a term or condition of instruction, employment, or participation in University activity; when submission to or rejection of such conduct by an individual is used as a basis for evaluation in making academic or personnel decisions affecting an individual; or when such verbal or physical conduct has the effect of unreasonably interfering with an individual's work, academic performance, or living conditions by creating an intimidating, hostile, or offensive environment.[15]

Sexual insults and prejudicial acts are intolerable, but most shocking are the physical assaults against women, which were reported on nearly a third of the campuses we visited. There was, for example, a widely publicized fraternity gang rape on one, and at another university 20 percent of the women surveyed reported having had unwanted sexual intercourse.[16]

In response, most colleges have focused on security *and* education. Colorado College, for example, offers free self-defense classes for women and provides them with whistles, while the State University of New York, Brockport, like many institutions, has installed "blue light" telephones around campus and initiated a student escort patrol.

At many colleges, "Take Back the Night" rallies have been organized, and health centers sensitize students to date rape. At the

University of Richmond, a mandatory session at freshman orientation includes skits that address what's called the "Triple Whammy" of drugs, sex, and alcohol. And women's centers are helpful, too. The University of Minnesota has one of the nation's oldest and best-established centers. Programs include counseling for those who have been sexually harassed and abused both on and off campus. There are meetings for older students, support groups for minority women, and a speaker series featuring artists, authors, and activists. Such actions deserve strong support on every campus.

Finally, women's studies programs, which seek to improve campus climate through education, have made impressive gains, increasing from a handful in the early 1970s to more than five hundred today. Such courses, which cut across the disciplines, share a common intellectual interest in the role of gender in society, in science, in literature, and the arts. We conclude that if women are to participate, without prejudice, in campus life, colleges must not only welcome them into the classroom, but into the curriculum.

A just community is a place where diversity is aggressively pursued. In the coming decade colleges and universities must commit themselves to increase the enrollment of minority students so that their participation in higher education at least matches their representation in the population.

But tolerance, in the sense of inclusion, is simply not enough. Martha Minow, professor of law at Harvard University, has observed that: "To many people who have been made marginal in the past, inclusion sounds like, 'come on in, but don't change anything.'"[17] The larger goal for higher education must be to "build academic communities in which people learn to respect and value one another for their differences, while at the same time defining the values shared by all those who join the university as scholars and as citizens."[18]

This vision of the college or university as a just community must be aggressively pursued, since it is becoming increasingly apparent that time is running out.

CHAPTER 4

A Disciplined Community

FOURTH, *a college or university is a* disciplined *community, a place where individuals accept their obligations to the group and where well-defined governance procedures guide behavior for the common good.*

A community of learning, at its best, is guided by standards of student conduct that define acceptable behavior and integrate the academic and nonacademic dimensions of campus life. We found, however, that when it comes to regulations, students live in two separate worlds. In academic matters, requirements are spelled out in great detail. Undergraduates are told how many graduation "units" to complete. They're given a schedule dictating when to show up for class, and they receive firm deadlines for term papers. But when it comes to life outside the classroom, the strategy is reversed. In nonacademic matters, standards are ambiguous, at best, and what we found particularly disturbing is the ambivalence college administrators feel about their overall responsibility for student behavior.

In just thirty years colleges have gone from being parents to clinicians, and today many are not sure where the oversight responsibility of the institution begins and ends. Many of us remember the days when there were enforced study hours and early lights out, except on weekends. We also can remember the sea change that occurred in the 1960s when too-rigid rules, belatedly, were abolished. No one would argue that colleges can or should return to the days of tight control. But does this mean that there are no standards by which conduct can be measured? Does it mean that colleges have no obligation to define with clarity their expectations for the students in matters beyond the academic?

Consider alcohol abuse. Pushed to the wall by legal and social factors, colleges are being forced to reappraise the legendary college figure of the boozing, boisterous undergraduate. Two-thirds of today's presidents called alcohol abuse a problem on their campuses. ''Substance abuse, primarily alcohol'' was mentioned most frequently when presidents were asked, ''What three campus-life issues have given you the greatest concern?''[1] Further, in a recent Carnegie survey of faculty, 33 percent of those responding said that alcohol abuse by students has increased.[2]

TABLE 5

Percentage of Presidents Who Rate Alcohol Abuse
a ''Moderate'' to ''Major'' Problem on Their Campus

All Institutions	Research & Doctorate-Granting	Comprehensive	Liberal Arts	Two-Year
67%	82%	84%	75%	53%

SOURCE: The Carnegie Foundation for the Advancement of Teaching and the American Council on Education, National Survey of College and University Presidents, 1989.

A recent University of Michigan study found that the reported use of illegal drugs by college students has gone down, from 56 percent in 1980 to 37 percent in 1989, but clearly substance abuse remains a serious concern.[3] At a prestigious southern university, we were told that drinking is the most popular ''unofficial student activity'' on campus.[4] The dean of students, who estimated that between 6 and 10 percent of undergraduates on his campus were alcoholics, speculated that another 30 to 40 percent were serious weekend drinkers.[5]

No one underestimates the difficulty of fighting alcohol abuse. Men and women proudly drinking to excess is as old as Bacchus and Beowulf. On campus, alcohol also has a long history of public acceptance and public consumption—from faculty sherry hours to fraternity beer parties. It's also true that many undergraduates have experience with alcohol and drugs long before they come to college.

38

TABLE 6

Campus Life Issues of Greatest Concern
Listed Most Frequently by Presidents
(Open-ended Question)

Substance Abuse (primarily alcohol)

Student Apathy

Campus Security and Crime

Inadequate Facilities

Interracial/Intercultural Relations

SOURCE: The Carnegie Foundation for the Advancement of Teaching and the American
Council on Education, National Survey of College and University Presidents,
1989.

Many others, leaving home for the first time, are eager to exercise
their new-found freedom, and social drinking and drug use fit in
perfectly with this desire.

Still, we conclude that clearly stated alcohol and drug policies are
required. If state laws say alcohol use is illegal for those under
twenty-one, colleges should make this fact clearly known to students
and declare that it will support the law, rather than ignore it. Such a
stand is not only a legal mandate, it is in the interest of the students,
too. They need models of integrity, not equivocation.

Colleges and universities are, in fact, responding to the crisis of
drug and alcohol abuse in a variety of ways. Some institutions,
especially those in states where the legal age for drinking has been
raised, have banned alcohol altogether. Others insist that it be served
only in designated places, while still other colleges now require
students to wear wrist bands or badges to identify their age. A few
places issue ''drink tickets'' to limit consumption and many require
that when alcohol is served, nonalcoholic drinks also be made
available at all college functions.

When rules are tightened, undergraduates often go off campus to
drink. A private Southwest university in our study passed a rule

forbidding all alcohol consumption on campus. In response, students presented an ultimatum: "If we can't drink on campus, we'll drive drunk"—a position the administrator called "blackmail." The moratorium was lifted but the university ruled that a uniformed police officer and four nondrinking chaperones must be present at all parties where alcohol is served.

Above all, education about the dangers of excessive drinking is important. Today, well over 90 percent of all colleges and universities have alcohol education programs, and more than 70 percent are making special efforts to reduce substance abuse.[6] Counselors, health officers, and chaplains are widely available on campus. We consider it quite remarkable that higher education institutions—in addition to academic, social, and residential programs—offer such a wide range of psychological support. And we were greatly impressed by the creative steps campuses are taking to hold off potential crises.

Each April, Indiana University holds a famous bike race—the Little 500—the biggest social weekend of the year. In 1988 the event was followed by a rock-throwing melee involving drunken students at an off-campus apartment complex. Students were arrested. For the 1989 festivities, the university scheduled extra entertainment events to discourage excessive drinking. Free bus service was also provided so students would not have to drive. Local bar owners offered free nonalcoholic beverages to designated drivers. A possible crisis was averted.

While campuses are safer than city streets, the frequency of criminal acts, for many colleges, is another cause for worry. Indeed, one in four of the student affairs officers responding to our survey say that the number of reported crimes on their campus has increased over the last five years. Forty-three percent of those responding at research and doctorate-granting institutions believe the number of reported crimes on campus has increased over the last five years.[7] One liberal arts college in our study reported a 27 percent rise in vandalism in just one year.[8] Thefts are considered a problem by about two-thirds of the presidents at doctorate-granting institutions; 38 percent of liberal arts college presidents; and 44 percent at two-year institutions.[9]

40

TABLE 7

Five-Year Change in Campus Crime
As Perceived by Student Affairs Officers
(Percentage Responding "Increase")

	All Institutions	Research & Doctorate-Granting	Compre-hensive	Liberal Arts	Two-Year
Number of reported crimes on campus	26%	43%	35%	32%	16%
Severity of crimes on campus	14	20	16	14	11
Number of reported crimes in surrounding community	50	59	54	42	49
Severity of crimes in surrounding community	41	56	46	30	41

SOURCE: The American Council on Education and the National Association of Student Personnel Administrators, National Survey of Chief Student Affairs Officers, 1989.

TABLE 8

Percentage of Presidents Who Say Crime Is a
"Moderate" to "Major" Problem on Their Campus

	All Institutions	Research & Doctorate-Granting	Compre-hensive	Liberal Arts	Two-Year
Thefts	47%	63%	57%	38%	44%
Inadequate security	38	34	34	41	39
Vandalism and destruction of property	36	56	44	36	29

SOURCE: The Carnegie Foundation for the Advancement of Teaching and the American Council on Education, National Survey of College and University Presidents, 1989.

We also found a close connection between alcohol abuse and campus crime. One administrator reported that 80 percent of all cases heard by the student judiciary at his institution were alcohol related. Still another told us that the recent increase in vandalism on his campus was caused by excessive drinking. The head of security at a midwestern land-grant university told one of our researchers: "The majority of crime on this campus comes from too much drinking."

Further, contrary to conventional wisdom, most criminal activity on campus is committed not by "outsiders" but by students. Students are, according to a recent report, responsible for 78 percent of sexual assaults, 52 percent of physical assaults, two-thirds of strong-arm robberies, more than 90 percent of arsons, and 85 percent of incidents of vandalism.[10]

What everyone fears most, of course, are crimes of violence. Despite the shocking headlines that report rape and murder, the campus is still a relatively safe place to be. But the problem is growing, especially for urban institutions. At one residential college, students told us it's just not safe to move about at night, and the dean of students advised those living in high-rise dormitories not to ride the elevators alone. At an urban university where several murders have occurred, students joke, with gallows humor, about living long enough to get their diplomas.

In 1986, a university student in Pennsylvania was raped and strangled in her dorm. The parents sued. An out-of-court settlement was reached when the university agreed to invest in improved lighting and other security precautions. The state legislature, responding to this and other incidents, passed a bill requiring every college and university in the state to publish its campus crime rates. Other states have enacted, or are considering, similar legislation. These anecdotes, while exceptions, reflect the levels of concern about campus safety.

Once again, we found that colleges and universities are moving aggressively to improve security—with better lighting, escort services, emergency phone systems, and a strengthened police force. One eastern university actually established a state-certified police academy on campus to train its own recruits. Student security patrols supervised by campus police also are widely used. And a northeastern university we visited has an "Operation ID" program to mark and register personal property. This, too, is becoming commonplace.

A few years ago, the University of Rochester hired a full-time staff member to direct its crime-prevention programs. The university now employs two full-time and two part-time people who conducted 120 crime-prevention seminars in one year. Rochester also has an "Operation ID" property identification, and about four years ago launched a Blue Light Escort Service in which students accompany colleagues at night. Working with the Women's Caucus, the community began a series of "Walks for Light," a project in which students and staff go around campus at night with security officials to identify places needing improved lighting. Twenty-two blue light phones and fifteen service phones have been added.

Every campus should have a comprehensive security plan, and we urge that during orientation all incoming students participate in a crime-awareness program. Residence hall leaders and other campus officials should offer seminars on safety, date rape, and the art of self-defense throughout the year. Academic departments should discuss safety issues with faculty and students, focusing especially on the use of facilities at night.

Finally, to give overall direction to campus life, all campuses should have a clearly stated code of conduct, one that is widely disseminated and consistently enforced. In our national survey of undergraduates, about half said they support a code of conduct; at liberal arts colleges it was 60 percent. The same percentage of undergraduates at liberal arts colleges said that known drug offenders should be suspended or dismissed. This was a dramatic increase from 1976. Sixty-six percent of the students also agreed that the drinking age in all states should be raised to twenty-one.[11]

In drawing up a campus code, simple courtesy and the rights of others must be affirmed. For example, privacy should be respected, and excessively loud noise should be restricted. And we also urge that every campus should involve faculty and students in the periodic review and update of campus codes. Such involvement provides an

TABLE 9

Undergraduate Attitudes Toward Moral Issues on Campus
(Percentage Agreeing)

	All Institutions	Research	Doctorate-Granting	Compre-hensive	Liberal Arts	Two-Year
Colleges should provide a code of conduct for students	56%	44%	47%	49%	60%	67%
Undergraduates known to use illegal drugs should be suspended or dismissed	56	51	52	55	62	59
Drinking age should be 21 in all states	66	51	58	64	64	74

SOURCE: The Carnegie Foundation for the Advancement of Teaching, National Survey of Undergraduates, 1984.

important opportunity to reaffirm the institution's commitment to high standards in all aspects of campus life.

Chancellor Kenneth R. R. Gros Louis at Indiana University, Bloomington, described the responsibility of the university this way:

> We must not back down in our attempts to create a climate in which the fundamental business of learning can go on unimpeded. We must make sure that we can guarantee basic needs and services, that we see the loss of personal safety—whether we mean sexual harassment or assault, racial harassment or assault, or even as mundane a violation as bicycle theft—as, at the least, a basic assault—a personal, individual violation of the rights that we all have as citizens, as students, as faculty and staff.[12]

On many of the campuses we visited administrators are, in fact, working closely with students to shape new rules regarding quiet hours, security procedures, the use of appliances, and parking restrictions, for example. More than half of the chief student affairs officers say that during the past five years student conduct regulations have become more explicit and enforcement more systematic. This pattern held true for all types of institutions, but it was highest at liberal arts colleges and research universities, where almost two-thirds of the student affairs officers report that such actions have been taken.[13]

TABLE 10

Student Affairs Officers' Views on the
Five-Year Change in Regulation of Student Conduct

	All Institutions	Research & Doctorate-Granting	Compre-hensive	Liberal Arts	Two-Year
More explicit	54%	63%	55%	66%	48%
About the same	45	37	45	31	52
Less explicit	1	0	0	3	0
More systematic enforcement	54	61	65	68	40
About the same	44	38	34	27	59
Less systematic enforcement	2	1	1	5	1

SOURCE: The American Council on Education and the National Association of Student Personnel Administrators, National Survey of Chief Student Affairs Officers, 1989.

In the end, a campus code of conduct should define standards of behavior in both social and academic matters. And yet there is disturbing evidence that here, too, behavior is deficient. Fraternities have long been known to keep old term papers on file for their members to copy, and it is possible for students to purchase papers on almost any topic from unscrupulous commercial organizations. Further, various surveys reveal that anywhere from 40 percent to nearly 90 percent of students cheat on tests or papers,[14] and 43 percent of today's faculty feel students are ready to cheat in order to get better grades.[15]

Faculty members are the first line of defense in holding students to high academic standards. And yet a recent study showed that 53 percent of faculty said they rarely or never discussed university procedures on dishonesty with students.[16] And a report from one university revealed that while nearly 60 percent of the faculty observed students cheating, only 20 percent actually met with the student and the departmental chairman, as called for in the university's code of conduct.[17]

We conclude that a college or university must be a *disciplined* community, a place where there are appropriate rules governing campus life, an institution where individuals acknowledge their obligations to the group. Specifically, we suggest an Honor Code for both the scholarly *and* the civic dimensions of campus life. Such codes convey a powerful message about how honesty and integrity form the foundation of a community of learning. Further, procedures for investigating and disciplining offenders must be in place.

Just as in social matters, all universities or colleges should have clear standards governing academic conduct, and all students on entrance must be absolutely clear about those policies and standards. The goal is not to have a list of unenforceable commandments. Rather, it is to assure that all parts of college life are governed by high standards.

CHAPTER 5

A Caring Community

FIFTH, *a college or university is a* caring *community, a place where the well-being of each member is sensitively supported and where service to others is encouraged.*

While colleges should be *purposeful,* and *just,* and *disciplined*—as well as *open*—the unique characteristic that makes these objectives work, the glue that holds it all together, is the way people relate to one another. As impossible as the goal may seem to be, a modern college or university should be a place where every individual feels affirmed and where every activity of the community is humane. Caring is the key.

At first blush, the term ''caring'' seems soft, almost sentimental. Yet, as human beings we have an absolute need for social bonding, from the first to the last moments of our lives. Professor Mary Clark, San Diego State University, puts the matter this way: ''Social bonds,'' she writes, ''are not temporary contracts entered into simply for the convenience of an individual, but are absolute requirements for human existence. Social embeddedness,'' Clark concludes, ''is the essence of our nature.''[1]

Students cherish their independence and accept as commonplace a campus environment that is more open, more relaxed. But undergraduates, like the rest of us, still need to feel that they belong. One student captured this paradox when she said, ''We don't want the university to be involved *in* our lives, but we would like someone to be concerned occasionally *about* our lives.''

We found, however, that at all too many institutions the connections students feel are tenuous, at best. No one expects the modern campus to have the intimacy of a family. Students are older, living self-directed lives. Yet, when we surveyed undergraduates several years ago, we were troubled to discover that about 50 percent said they "feel like a number in a book." About 40 percent said they do not feel a sense of community on campus, and about two-thirds said they have no professor "interested in their personal lives."[2]

And last year over three-quarters of college presidents we surveyed rated the lack of student involvement as one of the most serious campus life problems they confront. At two-year institutions it was 82 percent.[3]

TABLE 11

Percentage of Presidents Who Rate Nonparticipation by Students in Events a "Moderate" to "Major" Problem on Their Campus

	All Institutions	Research & Doctorate-Granting	Compre-hensive	Liberal Arts	Two-Year
Few students participate in campus events	76%	52%	78%	70%	82%

SOURCE: The Carnegie Foundation for the Advancement of Teaching and the American Council on Education, National Survey of College and University Presidents, 1989.

Many students, perhaps most, experience the academic community in only marginal and momentary ways. The common ground they share with others is the wish to get ahead, the goal of getting a credential, acquiring a degree. As a sophomore at a huge university in the Southwest said: "Yes, I think of this school as a community. People have common goals. Everyone's here to get a degree."

Students did, however, cite with satisfaction their membership in sororities and fraternities, the women's center, the student union, the newspaper, sports teams, the radio club, and the jazz club—groups that helped them feel connected. Students also spoke of connecting through living-learning centers, and through academic majors and clubs. And we were struck by the frequency with which students at

48

two-year institutions spoke of experiencing community at their institution, places that often were described as "truly caring."

Many faculty and administrators, especially those at large universities, feel that campus subgroups—such as those we've just cited—are the prerequisite for a healthy community. They argue that it's too much to expect students to feel bonded to a sprawling campus. A political scientist at a large western institution remarked: "Loyalty to the big institution develops only after these little loyalties." Even at colleges with smaller enrollments, most loyalties are formed to subgroups first. A student at a liberal arts college of eighteen hundred students echoed this view: "You can't have a community of the whole without the smaller groups."

Still, as we went from place to place, we also encountered concern about the negative influence of "little loyalties." There's a feeling, as we mentioned earlier, that the very organizations that give security to students can also create isolation and even generate friction on the campus. Fraternities and sororities, we found, are especially inclined to separate themselves too much from others for the wrong reasons.

When we asked college and university presidents about Greek life on their campus, more than half at research and doctorate institutions cited it as a problem.[4] The head of the Panhellenic Council at a small university in the Northeast put it this way: "The freshmen who rush want a place to belong. I joined a sorority because I had no girlfriends. I wanted some friends but Greeks form a sense of community for themselves."[5]

The problem of Greek houses, especially fraternities, is not just isolation, it's also bad behavior. At one liberal arts college that is 30 percent Greek, the faculty recommended disaffiliation to the Board of Trustees on three separate occasions, and cited the use and sale of drugs and alcohol abuse as cause. Even the President of the National Interfraternity Conference, a confederation of fifty-nine fraternities, spoke of the crisis: "Chapters that have gone undisciplined for years now resent our discussion of basic standards and expectations. They cannot begin to relate to our dialogues about 'values and ethics' of fraternity membership."[6]

TABLE 12

Percentage of Presidents Who Say Fraternities and Sororities Are a "Moderate" to "Major" Problem on Their Campus

All Institutions	Research & Doctorate-Granting	Comprehensive	Liberal Arts	Two-Year
19%	54%	34%	25%	3%

SOURCE: The Carnegie Foundation for the Advancement of Teaching and the American Council on Education, National Survey of College and University Presidents, 1989.

A college or university is diminished when students divide themselves, prejudicially, from one another or engage in destructive behavior, and unless Greeks function as purposeful, just, open, disciplined, and caring organizations, unless they commit themselves to supporting the larger purposes of the institution, they have no place in higher education. Recently, the Board of Directors of the American Council on Education adopted guidelines which stated: "As colleges and universities intensify their efforts to make their campuses hospitable to all groups, Greek organizations must take an active role in ensuring that their values and behaviors contribute to a positive campus life."[7] This should be the guiding principle for all groups on the campus.

Looking at the larger picture, we conclude that while subgroups on campus are important, they are not sufficient. As the vice-chancellor of a western university put it: "There is a great deal of 'orbital energy' among the many subgroups, a magnetism that tugs at these groups, pulling them away from any common agenda." In today's world students must connect with the institution as a whole, and we were encouraged to discover that chief administrators on campus say that strengthening community is a top priority for them; only 13 percent of the presidents we surveyed feel that "community can be sustained only in small groups or units."[8] The need, on campus—and in society—is for something more.

TABLE 13

Presidents Who Say Community Can Be
Sustained Only for Small Groups
(Percentage Agreeing)

All Institutions	Research & Doctorate-Granting	Comprehensive	Liberal Arts	Two-Year
13%	7%	9%	2%	19%

SOURCE: The Carnegie Foundation for the Advancement of Teaching and the American Council on Education, National Survey of College and University Presidents, 1989.

Creating a caring community takes on special significance for older students, who often march to a different drummer. Many hurry on and off the campus as they try to juggle work and family obligations. And we found that presidents are especially concerned about their inability to serve "commuter" students. Inadequate services for commuters was, in fact, rated a problem by about 60 percent of presidents at all four-year institutions. Even at community colleges, where virtually all students commute, about one-third of the presidents defined inadequate service for commuter students as a problem.[9]

Student affairs officers are worried, too. Thirty-six percent of those we surveyed said that "inadequate facilities for commuter students" was a greater problem today than five years ago. Over two-thirds rated "expanded services for nontraditional students" as "very important" for improving campus life.[10] The part-time students are, as one administrator put it, "on the edge of campus life."

At an urban university in our study, everything closes at 5:00 P.M. and at a rural community college, where almost all students commute, the counseling center is the only office open in the evening—the cafeteria, the bookstore, and the business offices are not. One student

TABLE 14

Percentage of Presidents Who Report Service to Commuter Students
Is a "Moderate" to "Major" Problem on Their Campus

All Institutions	Research & Doctorate-Granting	Comprehensive	Liberal Arts	Two-Year
45%	58%	56%	60%	32%

SOURCE: The Carnegie Foundation for the Advancement of Teaching and the American Council on Education, National Survey of College and University Presidents, 1989.

commented on this lack of caring when she said, "Here they seem to be worried only about my money."

We did find that extended office hours, counseling services, and day-care centers have been introduced on many campuses to help commuters. Student affairs staff, in particular, understand just how important it is for students of all ages to receive support, especially students on the margins. These professionals are the people who often put a human face on the institution. Many of the students sense that programs created by student affairs staff—in student unions, in residence halls, and in counseling centers—provide caring outside the classroom. We urge that such services be expanded, and well supported, by every institution.

At California State University, Dominguez Hills, an administrator, describes their program this way: "Our campus is open from eight in the morning to ten at night. We have a lot of support systems for older students to ensure graduation, such as a free learning center with computers for everything from math and physics to English. We also have advisement from the Educational Opportunity office on Saturdays. We've designed the programs to help the students, not to make our employees comfortable."

Piedmont Virginia Community College keeps offices open until 7:00 P.M. Administrators also serve on rotation so that one is available until 9:00 P.M. every evening. At the University of Louisville's ACCESS program all major campus services—admissions, registration, financial aid, career planning, and placement—have office hours until 8:00 P.M., and on Saturday morning, too. There is also a lounge and study area available for commuters.

But it's in the classroom where social and intellectual bonding is most likely to occur. For commuter students this is the primary point of campus contact, and community colleges are, we discovered, especially good at building a spirit of community among students. The classroom can be an oasis of social and emotional support in the often hectic lives of older students. At community colleges we heard students speak with gratitude about professors who gave them suggestions about books or articles to read, who spoke with them after class about ideas to consider, and even discussed personal plans and life choices.

A young woman student at Montgomery County Community College in Pennsylvania told a member of our staff: "Before I came, I was told, you will love MCCC. The professors are terrific. They spend a lot of time with you. That is so true. You will never find such a family environment as you will find here. The faculty have been very helpful. I have never been turned away when I went for advice." Another student at a community college described her instructors as people "who truly cared."

In reflecting on the impact of community colleges we were reminded that the spirit of community must be measured, not by the length of time on campus, but the quality of caring. It's how a student thinks and feels about a place that matters most, and even students who come to campus just several hours a week will feel part of a community if there is a supportive climate in the classroom, if they are treated with dignity by registrars and financial aid officers and the like, and if the office hours are arranged to serve the needs of students, not the system.

Finally, in a caring community, students should make a connection between what they learn and how they live. A college is a humane enterprise and it is more than mere sentiment to suggest that its quality depends upon the heads and the hearts of the individuals in it. The goal of educators should be to help students see that they are not only autonomous individuals but also members of a larger community to which they are accountable. Specifically, we urge that all students be encouraged to complete a community service project as an integral part of the undergraduate experience.

We are especially concerned that students reach out to others—to children and to older people to build bridges across the generations. Students also should be brought in touch with those genuinely in need, and through field experiences, build relationships that are intergenerational, intercultural, and international, too. In the end, the campus should be viewed not only as a place of introspection, but also as a staging ground for action.

At a time when social bonds are tenuous, students during their collegiate years should discover the reality of their dependence on each other. They must understand what it means to share and understand the benefits of giving. Community must be built. Thus, a caring community not only enables students to *gain* knowledge, but helps them channel that knowledge to humane ends.

54

CHAPTER 6

A Celebrative Community

SIXTH, *a college or university is a* celebrative *community, one in which the heritage of the institution is remembered and where rituals affirming both tradition and change are widely shared.*

If community in higher education is important—and almost all campus leaders agree that it is—colleges should sustain a keen sense of their own heritage and traditions. Old yearbooks with their depictions of white-glove and black-tie events or May Day ceremonies seem quaint today, and some rituals have lost their meaning. Still, rites, ceremonies, and celebrations unite the campus and give students a sense of belonging to something worthwhile and enduring. Celebrations, if meaningfully designed, sustain the vitality of campuses. The challenge is to instill all rituals and ceremonies with real significance—and fun as well. Such activities—and almost all colleges have their own unique traditions—show how memories can be kept alive and a sense of community can be sustained from year to year. Community must not only be created but recreated continually in institutions of higher education, and ritual has a vital role to play. These celebrations are critical, because from a quarter to a half of the undergraduates are new to a college each fall, and without traditions, continuity is lost.

Freshman orientation has long provided a splendid moment to introduce traditions, but on far too many campuses orientation was trivialized. The president and key academic officers were not involved, and it was left to the student personnel staff, almost exclusively, to help students become full members of the community of learning. But even then the focus was far more on the social than the academic.

The good news is that some colleges now have semester-long orientation seminars that highlight the heritage of the college in a richer, fuller sense. Orientation topics include not only a review of rules and regulations, and the hazards of alcohol and drug abuse, but also how and why the college was founded, the purpose of general education, the stories of the heroes of the institution, and the history behind the names on campus buildings.

Special freshman convocations can also highlight the culture of the campus and underscore coming to college as a special rite of passage. Colleges celebrate with students when their academic program is completed. Why not pause at the beginning, too? City College of the City University of New York, with its twenty thousand students, has a New Student Convocation. In this celebrative event, members of the faculty dress in academic garb, and the president talks about City College's academic heritage and honors senior professors who have been outstanding teachers. One recent awardee, in his remarks to new students, made this connection: "What most of you and I have in common," he said, "is that we were the first in our families to go to college. My parents didn't even finish grade school. They weren't even sure that I should go to college because they thought that perhaps I should make my living unloading trucks, next to my father."[1] The faculty and freshmen shared a bond of hope and courage.

Each fall the University of California at Berkeley welcomes students, faculty, and staff with a convocation, replete with refreshments and music. An academic procession wends its way into the Greek Theater. At a different event, the Fall Reception, each new student is greeted by a member of the university's faculty or staff and accompanied through a formal receiving line at the student union, where they meet Berkeley's chancellor. Then the new student is introduced to a senior who becomes his or her host.

Xavier University in New Orleans, which sustains a special feel of community, uses its Founder's Day convocation to celebrate the institution's special mission of serving blacks and other minorities who have been denied educational opportunities. At this campuswide celebration early each fall, outstanding faculty and students are

56

honored, seniors are recognized, new student leaders are inaugurated, and service awards are presented to faculty and staff.[2]

Students at Miami University—and other institutions as well—have a "Little Sibs" weekend to introduce their younger sisters and brothers to the campus. This weekend offers "little sibs" a first-hand opportunity to see what life on campus is like. For the students, the role of guide is a chance to renew their own ties to their community and culture. Siblings at Miami get to see and learn about the school's popular traditions such as the Miami bike race, alumni weekend, avoiding "stepping on the seal" (or you will fail your next exam), kissing in the Upham Arches, and the Western College "Shore to Slimy Shore Boat Race," in which teams design and race paper boats. Traditions like these are passed on to students in a number of ways—from their alumni parents, during tours of the campus, and at orientation and other freshman activities. These traditions all affirm the excitement and the variety of opportunities available for every student, and encourage their participation in the larger life of the college.[3]

Beyond fall orientation, colleges and universities can create on campus a climate of continuous bonding. At Evergreen State College, for example, faculty host potlucks in their homes, and retreats are held at The Farmhouse (a small lodge) at the Organic Farm. At the end of each academic year Evergreen celebrates Super Saturday. This event was initiated by a former Dean of Students and is a chance to thank everyone for another year. Super Saturday has grown to include a street fair, entertainment on three stages, two beer gardens, barbecues, and a "Friends of the Library" book sale, and it attracts nearly twenty-five thousand people. It not only brings the campus together, but also provides a unique opportunity to build goodwill between the college and the larger community.[4]

Another form of celebration can be less tangible, it's something "in the air." The intellectual accomplishments of the institution, for example, can offer this kind of atmosphere, and on several campuses we visited, students expressed pride in their school's "academic reputation," calling it the inspiration that holds the place together. Here's how one student put it: "Our departments are ranked high.

The faculty win so many awards. This is such an amazing place. Everything here is part of the university. There is a community feeling, a sense of pride.'' Students from a southern university, also, proud of the intellectual quality of the institution, compared themselves favorably to the large public university close by, declaring themselves to be more serious students.

Colleges sometimes also celebrate their buildings. ''Old Mains'' often have an honorable history, and occasionally humorous legends worth telling and retelling. Buildings are often named to celebrate individuals important in the folklore of the institution. Their stories should be told. Special landmarks and beautiful spots on the campus also give distinctiveness to the institution. Knowing more about these legacies and landmarks adds to the sense of belonging students feel—they enhance a community.

Reverence for the beauty of Indiana University at Bloomington helps unite the campus and even though Herman B. Wells retired from the presidency of Indiana almost thirty years ago, stories still are told about how he would send architects back to their drawing boards to save a tree. Such stories, often told with zest and affection, underscore how the physical setting can be a source of informal celebration.

Commencements and alumni weekends surely can have a distinctive flair. At Montgomery County Community College in Pennsylvania, students know each spring that their degrees will be granted in a tent ceremony. The practice began when the college was still in its infancy, in the early 1970s, because there was no building on campus large enough to allow more than four hundred people to gather at once. Now, even though more accommodating facilities are available, the tradition of commencement in a tent behind College Hall persists.

At Princeton University alumni return en masse each spring to march in a parade with graduating seniors. Known as the ''P-rade,'' the procession is led by members of the 25th-year reunion class, followed by the oldest alumni, known as the ''Old Guard.'' Strung out behind the ''Old Guard'' are classes of more recent vintage, in descending order, with the seniors bringing up the rear. Carrying class banners and dressed in colorful costumes and special blazers to distinguish each class, the alumni and their families and the seniors—some ten thousand strong—march through the campus to Clarke Field. The ceremony binds the youngest graduates to the generations preceding them.

Perhaps no campus tradition is more celebrative than sports, and certainly there is much to be said for the role of athletics in higher education. On the playing field, students have been taught discipline and fair play, and athletics has contributed greatly to the spirit of community on campus as well, powerfully uniting students, faculty, and alumni behind a common passion. But over the last century in America, intercollegiate athletics has developed a life of its own, one that has often distorted values, focusing not on the enrichment of student life, but on money.

Almost a hundred years ago, Woodrow Wilson, as president of Princeton University, lamented the negative influence of football: "As far as colleges go, the sideshows have swallowed up the circus, and we in the main tent do not know what is going on."[5] The situation today, at many of our best-known institutions, is very much worse, so that whatever these colleges or universities gain from sports in the way of community and enrichment of students is overshadowed by what they lose in terms of the integrity and central mission of higher education.

Intercollegiate athletics must enrich the academic mission, not negate it, and we found, in our study, places where sports do still serve the students, not the other way around. We found institutions where sports are put in the proper perspective and where the predominant attitude toward athletics among the students is one of playfulness. For example, at Earlham College, students proudly deemphasize sports, and approach them with a jovial, fun-filled attitude. Here, where sports teams are called "The Fighting Quakers," the athletic director has even forfeited games because team members were consumed by academic projects.

We compare this playful attitude and sense of perspective to the big-time sports, where athletics means staggering amounts of money, multi-million dollar television contracts, and unbelievably aggressive recruitment of students, who become pawns in an unseemly saga as their agents guide them not through their academic programs, but (realistically for only a few) toward professional football and basketball teams. In this environment, the pressure is great for administrators and faculty alike to bend the academic rules to the breaking point. What should be playful, even if disciplined, becomes deadly serious and damaging to the fundamental purpose of the institution.

While it may be unrealistic to expect colleges and universities with a tradition of big-time sports to deemphasize athletics, still, it is reasonable to call for a return to the middle ground. When celebration becomes hype and hysteria, and when it leads to dishonesty and to the establishment of a double academic standard, when it no longer truly serves the students, then the time has come for an institution to reexamine its priorities and build its tradition on integrity, not abuse.

The celebrative community uses ceremony and ritual to recall the past, to affirm tradition and build larger loyalties on campus. But as colleges and universities become more richly inclusive, as the student body becomes more and more diverse, campuses should find ways to celebrate, not just tradition, but change and innovation as well.

We mentioned earlier the P-rade at Princeton. It's worth noting how the dynamics of that event are affected when the class that first opened its ranks to women marches along the parade route. There is cheering, dancing, and enthusiastic celebration of a significant change in the history of the university. In that same spirit colleges and universities should schedule special events throughout the year that highlight the rich contributions of the racial and ethnic groups on campus. Martin Luther King, Jr., Day, for example, should be honored and times also should be put aside to feature Hispanic, Asian, and Native American cultures. We urge, too, that the influence of women, nationally and within the institution, be a part of the celebrative community.

At Northern Arizona University, Honor Weeks 1989 was the scene for a host of distinguished speakers such as Wilma Mankiller, principal chief of Cherokee Nation of Oklahoma. The speakers all brought perspectives from culturally diverse populations. The event sent a special message that such speakers are not brought in just for Martin Luther King Day or *Cinco de Mayo*. Rather, it demonstrated that culturally diverse perspectives are an essential part of what everyone in the community needs to know.

Foreign students on campus also should be brought more significantly into the celebrative campus community. They provide colleges and universities with unique opportunities to create connections between students of dramatically different backgrounds, broadening the experience and learning of all. Too often, however, foreign students are isolated. Though they come together themselves for formal talks, discussions, and celebrations, with few exceptions students in the larger community remain uninformed by their contributions.

We are convinced that far more can and should be done, administratively, to tap this intellectual and cultural wealth of the international community on campus. Campuswide events—formal talks as well as festivities with food, music, and dance—should routinely take place every year so that large numbers of students could benefit from the presence of these students who come from all over the world. Further, international students should be viewed as a rich educational resource and be asked, from time to time, to give special lectures in classes, featured as a unique resource on the campus.

Older students, also, bring a wealth of experience to the campus community, but often remain detached from the mainstream of campus life. Again, community colleges, we found, frequently demonstrate a great commitment to older students, and plan events with their needs and contributions in mind. But for the most part, the experience that older students bring with them to campus is left unexplored and unappreciated. When older students are only tolerated instead of meaningfully included, an important part of the mission of higher education fails. Colleges and universities should, we believe, make a special effort to celebrate the diversity older students add to campus life, scheduling events and talks in which these students' perspectives and special needs are highlighted, and thereby teaching younger students to regard them with respect.

While leaving space for privacy and individual interests, we believe that a university at its best encourages people to share rituals and traditions that connect them to the campus community and that improve the civic culture and diversity of the institution. The academic mission and the integrity of the higher learning institution, as well as the diversity of people who make up the community, should inform all celebrations on campus, formal and informal, academic and athletic.

Compact for Community

A RINGING CALL FOR the renewal of community in higher learning may, at first, seem quixotic. Not only has cultural coherence faded, but the very notion of commonalities seems strikingly inapplicable to the vigorous diversity of contemporary life. Within the academy itself, the fragmentation of knowledge, narrow departmentalism, and an intense vocationalism are, as we have acknowledged, the strongest characteristics of collegiate education.

Still, we believe the undergraduate experience can, by bringing together the separate parts, create something greater than the sum, and offer the prospect that the channels of our common life will be renewed and deepened.

Students come to college to follow their own special aptitudes and interests. They are eager to get credentials and get a job, become productive, self-reliant human beings and, with new knowledge, continue to learn after college days are over. Serving the educational needs of each student must remain a top priority in higher education, but private concerns, while important, are insufficient.

Perhaps we can draw an analogy from a different field. Paul Goldberger, architecture critic for *The New York Times,* observed that while city life has always been characterized by a struggle between the private and public sectors, there was once general respect for buildings and spaces "of the public realm." In New York City, for example, this meant Central Park, Grand Central Terminal, the New York Public Library, the road, park, and tunnel systems. In recent years, however, commitment to the public realm diminished or, as Goldberger put it, commitment "to the very idea . . . that the city is a collective, shared place, a place that is in the most literal sense common ground."[1]

As the inspiration of shared spaces lost appeal—with people retreating increasingly into their own private worlds—many seemed to feel that the public domain in cities could not be reclaimed. Still, a city simply cannot function physically without an infrastructure—roadways, pipes and tunnels for water and waste, basic public services—nor can it survive spiritually without the spaces and places that sustain its intellectual, social, and artistic life.

So it is with higher education. The nation and the world need educated men and women who not only pursue their own personal interests but also are prepared to fulfill their social and civic obligations. And it is during the college years, perhaps more than at any other time, that these essential qualities of mind and character are refined.

The academic and social divisions that characterize the modern campus create a special need for common purposes to give meaning to the enterprise. And while higher education has a wide range of priorities to pursue, we are convinced that all parts of campus life can relate to one another and contribute to a sense of wholeness.

It is of special significance, we believe, that higher learning institutions, even the big, complex ones, continue to use the familiar rhetoric of "community" to describe campus life and even use the metaphor of "family." Especially significant, 97 percent of the college and university presidents we surveyed said they "strongly believe in the importance of community." Almost all the presidents agreed that "community is appropriate for my campus" and also support the proposition that "administrators should make a greater effort to strengthen common purposes and shared experiences."[2]

We proceed then with the conviction that if a balance can be struck between individual interests and shared concerns, a strong learning community will result. We believe the six principles highlighted in this report—purposefulness, openness, justice, discipline, caring, and celebration—can form the foundation on which a vital community of learning can be built. Now, more than ever, colleges and universities should be guided by a larger vision.

Building community in higher education calls for leadership at the highest level. The president sets the tone of the institution and, in large

TABLE 15

Presidents' Views on the Role of Community
(Percentage Responding "Agree")

	All Institutions	Research & Doctorate- Granting	Compre- hensive	Liberal Arts	Two- Year
Administrators should make a greater effort to strengthen common purposes and shared experiences	97%	96%	100%	99%	95%
I strongly believe in the importance of "community"	96	97	99	100	93
The idea of "community" is no longer appropriate for an institution such as this	4	0	4	0	7

SOURCE: The Carnegie Foundation for the Advancement of Teaching and the American Council on Education, National Survey of College and University Presidents, 1989.

measure, determines the priorities to be pursued. The president, as chief *administrator,* is engaged in the day-to-day details of management. But the task of the president as *leader* is to transcend details, present a larger, more inspired vision and remind the community of those essential qualities that guide the institution.

But how can the principles proposed in this report be converted into practice?

As a first step, the president may wish to convene a campuswide forum, or use existing forums such as the faculty senate or student assembly, to discuss the six principles and the idea of adopting them, more formally, as a campus *compact.* And we urge that trustees, early on, be brought into the discussion. The entire board could be engaged in a consideration of the principles of community and also ratify them as the framework to be used in shaping policy and practice.

To adopt the principles as a campus compact would signal the seriousness with which the enduring values of the institution were

65

understood and embraced. All members of the community would be reminded of their importance and, as a compact, the principles could be referred to, with authority, and passed on from one student generation to another.

The compact could be used by the president in working with his or her administrative team. Consider the possibility of a fall retreat in which key officials meet together for several days to discuss the six dimensions of community and use them as a way to assess the institution. For example, a report card might be prepared, one that evaluates current college performance against each principle and includes an action plan to improve campus life in those areas where the institution is judged deficient.

We also could imagine using the compact in orienting incoming students to the college and we could imagine, as well, a semester-long series of events in which one principle—a *just* community, for example—would be the subject of guest lecturers, faculty symposia, and student forums. Then another principle could be explored.

Further, with the six principles to guide the conversation, faculty and administrators could meet on common ground when academic policies are considered. Student personnel officers also might find the principles useful in resolving matters affecting student life. And could student, faculty, and administrative leaders use the principles to guide day-to-day decisions—from inviting speakers or entertainment groups, to planning courses, to academic evaluations and even hiring personnel?

They could be used also by administrators as a litmus test to evaluate the appropriateness of new student organizations—or to measure the worthiness of existing ones. A fraternity, for example, might be asked to assess the value of its programs by using purposefulness, openness, justice, discipline, caring, and celebration as the yardsticks of assessment.

Looking beyond the campus, accreditation bodies might use the compact in their assessment of the quality of a college or university. Instead of evaluating the institution on the basis of administrative functions—instructional, library, student services and the rest—could

66

the accreditation team apply the six principles to critique both academic and nonacademic actions?

Again, the president clearly has a crucial role to play in reminding all constituencies that the campus is being guided by high standards, not ad hoc arrangements. While affirming principles surely will not resolve all differences of opinion, it would, we believe, help lift the level of discourse and provide an appropriate framework within which campus decisions might be made.

But leadership means far more than inspired direction from the top. It also means assuring that decision making at all levels will be based on high standards that are widely shared. And it is our hope that the guidelines discussed in this report might provide the thread of a durable new compact, one in which students and faculty come together as scholars-citizens to create an organic community whose members are not only intellectually engaged, but also committed to civility on campus.

In the end, building a vital community is a challenge confronting not just higher learning, but the whole society. In our hard-edged competitive world, more humane, more integrative purposes must be defined. And perhaps it is not too much to hope that as colleges and universities affirm a new vision of community on campus, they may also promote the common good in the neighborhood, the nation, and the world.

APPENDICES

APPENDIX A

National Survey of College and University Presidents, 1989

TABLE A-1

Campus Life Issues of Greatest Concern
(Percentage of Presidents Listing Each Response)

	All Institutions	Research & Doctorate-Granting	Comprehensive	Liberal Arts	Two-Year
Substance abuse (primarily alcohol)	45%	51%	54%	50%	37%
Student apathy	30	12	20	23	43
Campus security and crime	25	31	30	19	24
Inadequate facilities	18	19	10	16	22
Interracial/intercultural relations	13	32	21	14	5
Adequacy of services and programming for commuter/nontraditional students	11	6	4	8	18
AIDS education and issues of human sexuality	9	8	7	7	11
Incivility, disrespect by students	9	5	3	9	14
Inadequate advising	8	4	6	0	13
Lack of student leadership	8	2	9	9	8
Student stress/dysfunction	7	10	2	13	6
Academic dishonesty, student values	7	8	10	10	5

TABLE A-1 *(cont.)*

	All Institutions	Research & Doctorate-Granting	Comprehensive	Liberal Arts	Two-Year
General lack of sense of campus community	7%	8%	7%	11%	5%
Quality of residential life	6	8	5	12	3
Vandalism	6	2	8	6	6
Recruitment/retention of minorities	5	9	2	5	6
Greek organizations	5	7	7	12	0
College costs/aid availability	4	11	6	2	2
Regulation of alcohol use, on and off campus	4	4	5	7	2
Lack of appreciation for differences	3	11	6	3	0
Budgetary constraints	3	9	3	3	2
Retention	3	1	7	2	2
Sexual harassment	2	2	3	4	0
Faculty-student interaction	2	2	2	3	2
Other	60	39	65	54	65

SOURCE: The Carnegie Foundation for the Advancement of Teaching and the American Council on Education, National Survey of College and University Presidents, 1989.

TABLE A-2

Extent of Problems Reported by Presidents
(Percentage Giving Each Response)

	All Institutions	Research & Doctorate-Granting	Comprehensive	Liberal Arts	Two-Year
Few students participate in campus events					
Major	14%	11%	11%	14%	15%
4	33	20	29	30	39
Moderate	29	21	38	26	28
2	16	36	19	22	10
Not a Problem	10	15	5	11	11
Inadequate facilities for campus gatherings					
Major	13	15	8	16	14
4	20	27	20	23	17
Moderate	22	18	24	21	22
2	19	27	24	21	15
Not a Problem	28	16	27	22	34

TABLE A-2 *(cont.)*

	All Institutions	Research & Doctorate-Granting	Comprehensive	Liberal Arts	Two-Year
Alcohol Abuse					
Major	11%	17%	15%	12%	7%
4	22	47	29	24	14
Moderate	34	18	40	39	32
2	20	17	11	22	24
Not a Problem	15	3	8	5	25
Overcrowded or outdated residence halls					
Major	9	11	10	15	3
4	9	19	11	15	2
Moderate	18	21	22	22	12
2	14	29	20	15	6
Not a Problem	54	23	40	35	80
Inadequate facilities for commuter students					
Major	7	10	8	7	6
4	14	19	17	15	12
Moderate	28	31	35	41	18
2	22	23	24	23	20
Not a Problem	32	19	20	17	47

TABLE A-2 *(cont.)*

	All Institutions	Research & Doctorate-Granting	Comprehensive	Liberal Arts	Two-Year
Inadequate services for commuter students					
Major	5%	7%	7%	6%	3%
4	12	11	17	13	10
Moderate	28	40	32	41	19
2	25	27	33	26	21
Not a Problem	32	18	13	17	50
Excessive noise and disruptiveness in campus residences					
Major	4	3	2	6	3
4	16	17	16	20	13
Moderate	29	39	41	39	15
2	23	38	29	27	15
Not a Problem	30	6	15	11	56
Thefts					
Major	3	2	2	3	4
4	10	16	7	9	11
Moderate	34	45	48	26	29
2	42	34	41	47	41
Not a Problem	14	3	5	18	18

TABLE A-2 (cont.)

	All Institutions	Research & Doctorate-Granting	Comprehensive	Liberal Arts	Two-Year
Drug/substance abuse					
Major	3%	3%	5%	2%	3%
4	7	13	8	9	4
Moderate	35	30	33	28	40
2	40	49	45	51	31
Not a Problem	17	8	11	13	24
Poor academic advising					
Major	2	9	2	2	2
4	12	26	20	7	8
Moderate	29	37	32	28	26
2	36	28	31	40	39
Not a Problem	23	3	18	26	27
Inadequate security					
Major	2	2	2	2	2
4	8	9	6	8	8
Moderate	28	23	26	31	29
2	32	51	33	43	24
Not a Problem	33	18	36	18	40

TABLE A-2 (cont.)

	All Institutions	Research & Doctorate-Granting	Comprehensive	Liberal Arts	Two-Year
Racial tensions/hostilities					
Major	2%	6%	3%	1%	1%
4	5	16	4	10	1
Moderate	17	46	13	17	13
2	39	29	43	41	39
Not a Problem	40	5	39	34	50
Greek life problems					
Major	2	5	1	5	1
4	5	14	9	8	1
Moderate	12	35	24	12	1
2	10	29	15	14	1
Not a Problem	74	20	54	64	101
Vandalism and destruction of property					
Major	1	0	2	1	2
4	8	9	5	11	7
Moderate	27	47	37	24	20
2	46	35	52	49	44
Not a Problem	20	9	7	18	30

TABLE A-2 (cont.)

	All Institutions	Research & Doctorate-Granting	Comprehensive	Liberal Arts	Two-Year
Crude and offensive behavior at sports events					
Major	1%	3%	2%	1%	1%
4	5	13	3	6	3
Moderate	9	17	13	11	5
2	31	39	43	36	20
Not a Problem	57	30	41	49	74
Sexual harassment					
Major	1	2	1	1	1
4	4	13	3	5	3
Moderate	23	47	28	24	16
2	46	36	55	46	43
Not a Problem	29	4	17	27	40
Violations of honor codes or rules of academic integrity					
Major	1	1	1	1	1
4	4	15	1	5	4
Moderate	21	31	23	30	14
2	43	43	58	43	37
Not a Problem	34	13	21	24	48

TABLE A-2 (cont.)

	All Institutions	Research & Doctorate-Granting	Comprehensive	Liberal Arts	Two-Year
Incidents involving physical violence					
Major	1%	1%	2%	2%	1%
4	4	5	4	5	4
Moderate	13	25	14	8	13
2	38	55	46	45	27
Not a Problem	46	17	37	43	58
Disruptive behavior by nonstudents					
Major	1	1	3	1	1
4	4	7	4	5	4
Moderate	13	18	13	11	12
2	29	37	38	38	19
Not a Problem	56	40	44	47	68
Rape/sexual assault					
Major	1	1	2	1	1
4	4	17	2	5	3
Moderate	9	32	12	13	2
2	34	35	51	38	24
Not a Problem	55	17	36	46	74

TABLE A-2 *(cont.)*

	All Institutions	Research & Doctorate-Granting	Comprehensive	Liberal Arts	Two-Year
Suicides and suicide attempts					
Major	1%	3%	1%	1%	2%
4	3	11	3	3	2
Moderate	14	29	25	19	4
2	40	43	47	46	33
Not a Problem	44	17	27	33	62
Racial intimidation/harassment					
Major	1	2	3	1	1
4	3	9	3	4	2
Moderate	12	37	12	10	10
2	36	44	39	42	31
Not a Problem	50	10	45	47	60
Lack of civility when disputes arise					
Major	1	2	1	3	1
4	3	4	3	4	3
Moderate	8	20	7	7	7
2	37	48	45	43	29
Not a Problem	53	29	47	46	63

TABLE A-2 (cont.)

	All Institutions	Research & Doctorate-Granting	Comprehensive	Liberal Arts	Two-Year
Excessive drinking at sports events					
Major	1%	6%	1%	1%	1%
4	3	13	2	3	2
Moderate	5	14	9	5	2
2	20	30	32	17	14
Not a Problem	73	39	59	77	84
Hazing incidents					
Major	1	2	1	1	1
4	2	4	2	6	1
Moderate	8	18	14	9	2
2	16	52	27	20	3
Not a Problem	76	26	59	67	97
Disruptive behavior at commencement or convocation ceremonies					
Major	1	2	1	1	1
4	1	3	1	3	1
Moderate	5	14	9	1	3
2	14	20	16	14	12
Not a Problem	82	64	76	84	87

TABLE A-2 *(cont.)*

	All Institutions	Research & Doctorate-Granting	Comprehensive	Liberal Arts	Two-Year
Incidents involving guns and other weapons					
Major	1%	1%	1%	1%	1%
4	1	1	1	1	2
Moderate	4	6	7	3	3
2	20	36	25	17	17
Not a Problem	77	60	70	82	80
Disruptive protest demonstrations					
Major	1	1	1	1	1
4	1	3	1	1	1
Moderate	1	8	1	1	1
2	8	31	13	7	3
Not a Problem	91	60	88	92	98
Other					
Major	21	31	70	14	11
4	11	31	1	1	12
Moderate	18	29	1	1	23
2	2	12	1	1	1
Not a Problem	52	1	31	87	56

SOURCE: The Carnegie Foundation for the Advancement of Teaching and the American Council on Education, National Survey of College and University Presidents, 1989.

TABLE A-3

Campus Life Issues in Context

(Percentage of Presidents Giving Each Response)

	All Institutions	Research & Doctorate-Granting	Comprehensive	Liberal Arts	Two-Year
Campus life problems are made more difficult by conditions in the larger society					
Yes	72%	85%	82%	86%	59%
No	22	8	16	7	34
Uncertain	6	7	3	7	7
The quality of campus life is of greater concern today, versus a few years ago					
Yes	52	58	46	58	52
No	38	36	42	37	36
Uncertain	10	6	12	5	11
Campus life problems are made more difficult by changes in the composition of the student body					
Yes	38	36	31	44	39
No	57	57	63	51	57
Uncertain	5	7	7	5	5

TABLE A-3 (cont.)

	All Institutions	Research & Doctorate-Granting	Comprehensive	Liberal Arts	Two-Year
Campus life problems are made more difficult by conditions in the surrounding community					
Yes	35%	53%	43%	32%	29%
No	58	44	52	61	61
Uncertain	7	3	5	8	9
Campus life problems are made more difficult by your campus's enrollment size					
Yes	27	29	20	24	31
No	69	65	75	70	66
Uncertain	4	6	5	6	3

SOURCE: The Carnegie Foundation for the Advancement of Teaching and the American Council on Education, National Survey of College and University Presidents, 1989.

TABLE A-4

Presidents' Views on Improving Campus Life
(Percentage Giving Each Response)

	All Institutions	Research & Doctorate-Granting	Comprehensive	Liberal Arts	Two-Year
Greater effort to build a stronger overall sense of community					
Very important	71%	87%	74%	79%	64%
Somewhat important	27	12	26	20	34
Not important	1	2	0	1	2
More interaction between students and faculty					
Very important	64	76	61	65	63
Somewhat important	34	24	38	29	35
Not important	3	0	1	5	2
Better campus communications					
Very important	60	58	53	47	69
Somewhat important	38	39	43	48	30
Not important	3	3	4	5	1

TABLE A-4 (cont.)

	All Institutions	Research & Doctorate-Granting	Comprehensive	Liberal Arts	Two-Year
More events that affirm the institution's mission, objectives, and values					
Very important	60%	71%	67%	65%	52%
Somewhat important	37	27	30	29	45
Not important	4	2	3	7	3
More events that bring large numbers of students, faculty, and staff together					
Very important	59	49	55	62	61
Somewhat important	35	47	43	32	30
Not important	7	4	2	6	9
Closer links between classroom and out-of-class activities					
Very important	56	64	48	72	51
Somewhat important	40	31	51	26	43
Not important	4	5	1	2	6

TABLE A-4 (cont.)

	All Institutions	Research & Doctorate-Granting	Comprehensive	Liberal Arts	Two-Year
Expanded services for nontraditional students					
Very important	50%	37%	55%	32%	57%
Somewhat important	39	53	39	48	34
Not important	11	11	5	20	9
Greater understanding and awareness of racial/ethnic diversity					
Very important	49	82	62	51	36
Somewhat important	40	18	34	38	47
Not important	11	0	4	11	17
More leadership opportunities for students					
Very important	47	35	49	40	51
Somewhat important	47	49	49	49	44
Not important	7	16	1	11	6

TABLE A-4 (cont.)

	All Institutions	Research & Doctorate-Granting	Comprehensive	Liberal Arts	Two-Year
Better orientation programs					
Very important	46%	36%	40%	34%	55%
Somewhat important	49	57	53	60	42
Not important	5	7	7	6	3
More aggressive programs to prevent alcohol and drug abuse					
Very important	45	60	52	44	40
Somewhat important	44	29	35	51	48
Not important	10	11	13	5	11
More explicit expectations for student behavior and responsibilities					
Very important	39	33	36	40	42
Somewhat important	50	57	51	51	49
Not important	10	9	14	10	9
Greater incentives for alcohol-free events					
Very important	39	51	50	33	34
Somewhat important	36	32	37	36	37
Not important	25	17	14	31	29

TABLE A-4 *(cont.)*

	All Institutions	Research & Doctorate-Granting	Comprehensive	Liberal Arts	Two-Year
More collaborative learning among students					
Very important	33%	22%	35%	25%	37%
Somewhat important	58	64	61	67	50
Not important	10	14	4	7	13
Workshops on conflict resolution					
Very important	23	15	19	18	28
Somewhat important	46	63	55	49	38
Not important	31	22	26	33	34
New or revised statements on civility and respect for others					
Very important	23	20	24	23	24
Somewhat important	44	66	43	43	42
Not important	33	14	33	34	35
Better enforcement of rules governing student behavior					
Very important	21	19	22	19	22
Somewhat important	55	66	64	59	48
Not important	24	15	14	22	31

TABLE A-4 (cont.)

	All Institutions	Research & Doctorate-Granting	Comprehensive	Liberal Arts	Two-Year
Better procedures for handling complaints and grievances					
Very important	21%	20%	23%	15%	24%
Somewhat important	52	59	57	62	43
Not important	27	21	20	23	33
Strengthened campus police force and security					
Very important	20	16	26	16	19
Somewhat important	55	57	48	58	56
Not important	26	27	26	26	25
Other					
Very important	46	85	0	0	50
Somewhat important	4	15	0	0	0
Not important	50	0	100	100	50

SOURCE: The Carnegie Foundation for the Advancement of Teaching and the American Council on Education, National Survey of College and University Presidents, 1989.

TABLE A-5

Most Positive Developments to Address Campus Life Issues
(Percentage of Presidents Listing Each Response)

	All Institutions	Research & Doctorate-Granting	Comprehensive	Liberal Arts	Two-Year
Active student government/greater student involvement	26%	12%	19%	15%	42%
Better campus communications	19	20	18	11	23
Increased awareness/commitment to improve campus life	12	19	16	13	8
New or expanded student activities programming	12	10	13	10	13
Able, effective student affairs personnel	10	9	16	8	8
Construction of student center or other campus facility for social gatherings	9	4	7	8	10
New/improved counseling program	9	3	4	9	13

TABLE A-5 *(cont.)*

	All Institutions	Research & Doctorate-Granting	Comprehensive	Liberal Arts	Two-Year
Development/redesign of orientation program or course	8%	7%	2%	14%	8%
Formal project/group commissioned to monitor quality of campus life	7	9	3	12	5
Improved administration or coordination of student services	6	10	15	2	3
Creation of alcohol/substance abuse program	6	9	5	10	3
Specific board/committee created	6	2	9	4	5
New student affairs personnel or senior administrator concerned with student life	5	8	2	6	5
Planned forums or other scheduled community events on campus life issues	5	4	2	6	8
Long-range planning	5	3	5	15	0
Specific policy/program created	4	5	4	9	0

TABLE A-5 (cont.)

	All Institutions	Research & Doctorate-Granting	Comprehensive	Liberal Arts	Two-Year
Leadership development program	4%	2%	5%	2%	5%
Existing committee structure	4	0	2	0	8
Renovation or construction of student housing	3	10	2	4	3
New policies, programs, or personnel in residence halls	3	8	3	6	0
Committee on the status of minorities and/or campus diversity	3	6	5	2	3
Attention to hiring and retention of minority students and faculty	3	4	0	1	5
New policies or programs affecting Greek organizations	2	2	2	4	0
New student organization formed	2	1	2	1	3

TABLE A-5 *(cont.)*

	All Institutions	Research & Doctorate-Granting	Comprehensive	Liberal Arts	Two-Year
Presidential leadership	1%	6%	0%	1%	0%
Enforcement of policies/practices	1	0	4	0	0
Greater effort to build community	1	0	2	3	0
Other	25	26	32	25	21

SOURCE: The Carnegie Foundation for the Advancement of Teaching and the American Council on Education, National Survey of College and University Presidents, 1989.

TABLE A-6

Most Important Actions to Improve Campus Life
(Percentage of Presidents Listing Each Response)

	All Institutions	Research & Doctorate-Granting	Comprehensive	Liberal Arts	Two-Year
Be visible and involved in campus events	39%	34%	32%	40%	45%
Be accessible to students, faculty and staff	27	23	33	21	26
Act as role model to communicate campus values and standards	23	24	28	29	16
Provide adequate facilities/staff for campus programs	19	9	18	22	21
Advocate for programs that improve campus life	17	31	7	19	18
Listen to and stay familiar with student and faculty concerns	17	9	16	24	16

TABLE A-6 *(cont.)*

	All Institutions	Research & Doctorate-Granting	Comprehensive	Liberal Arts	Two-Year
Affirm institutional mission, objectives and values	13%	16%	22%	14%	5%
Provide strong leadership	12	22	9	17	8
Support student services/affairs staff	12	12	13	15	11
Cultivate a sense of community	12	9	19	13	8
Enhance campus communication among students/faculty/staff/administrators	11	13	8	6	16
Hire qualified and innovative staff to address these issues	8	12	7	3	11
Support student government and/or other student organizations	8	5	7	4	11

TABLE A-6 *(cont.)*

	All Institutions	Research & Doctorate-Granting	Comprehensive	Liberal Arts	Two-Year
Acknowledge quality of campus life as a priority	7%	4%	6%	2%	11%
Encourage, reward faculty-student interaction	6	7	7	3	8
Enforce existing rules and regulations; discipline violators	5	8	10	9	0
Set institutional goals and provide funds to meet them	4	3	4	1	5
Encourage campus participation	4	2	3	4	5
Be proactive in identifying and addressing campus concerns	3	1	0	9	3
Ensure open discussion of campus issues	2	4	2	3	0

TABLE A-6 (cont.)

	All Institutions	Research & Doctorate-Granting	Comprehensive	Liberal Arts	Two-Year
Be open to divergent views	2%	0%	0%	2%	3%
Be knowledgeable of campus services	1	0	0	2	0
Be actively involved in faculty and staff hiring	1	0	0	0	3
Other	48	52	48	38	53

SOURCE: The Carnegie Foundation for the Advancement of Teaching and the American Council on Education, National Survey of College and University Presidents, 1989.

TABLE A-7

Presidents' Views on the Role of Community

(Percentage Giving Each Response)

	All Institutions	Research & Doctorate-Granting	Comprehensive	Liberal Arts	Two-Year
Administrators should make a greater effort to strengthen common purposes and shared experiences at their institutions.					
Agree	97%	96%	100%	99%	95%
Disagree	3	4	0	1	5
I strongly believe in the importance of "community" for an institution such as this.					
Agree	96	97	99	100	93
Disagree	4	3	1	0	7
"Community" is appropriate for my campus.					
Yes	91	92	95	97	86
No	1	2	0	0	2
Partly	8	6	5	3	12

TABLE A-7 *(cont.)*

	All Institutions	Research & Doctorate-Granting	Comprehensive	Liberal Arts	Two-Year
"Community" can be sustained only for small groups or units, not for this institution as a whole.					
Agree	13%	7%	9%	2%	19%
Disagree	87	93	91	98	81
The idea of "community" is no longer appropriate for an institution such as this.					
Agree	4	0	4	0	7
Disagree	96	100	96	100	93

SOURCE: The Carnegie Foundation for the Advancement of Teaching and the American Council on Education, National Survey of College and University Presidents, 1989.

APPENDIX B

National Survey of Chief Student Affairs Officers, 1989

TABLE B-1

Institutional Characteristics
(Percentage Giving Each Response)

	All Institutions	Research & Doctorate-Granting	Comprehensive	Liberal Arts	Two-Year
Institution is:					
Rural/small city	54%	31%	39%	64%	61%
Suburban	22	17	27	20	21
Urban	24	52	33	16	18
Primarily residential	33	48	34	71	14
Primarily commuter	57	31	45	16	85
Evenly divided	10	21	22	13	1

SOURCE: The American Council on Education and the National Association of Student Personnel Administrators, National Survey of Chief Student Affairs Officers, 1989.

TABLE B-2

Student Characteristics
(Percentage Giving Each Response)

	All Institutions	Research & Doctorate-Granting	Comprehensive	Liberal Arts	Two-Year
Percentage of all undergraduates:					
Over age 25					
Less than 10 percent	20%	26%	22%	43%	8%
10-24 percent	21	38	32	27	11
25-49 percent	25	26	25	21	26
50-74 percent	29	9	20	4	47
75 percent or more	5	1	1	5	7
Part-time students					
Less than 10 percent	21	30	21	41	10
10-24 percent	23	44	36	32	9
25-49 percent	19	20	27	20	15
50-74 percent	30	6	15	5	53
75 percent or more	7	0	1	2	13
In residence halls					
Less than 10 percent	41	6	26	7	77
10-24 percent	11	27	15	8	7
25-49 percent	14	35	22	12	6
50 percent or more	34	31	37	74	10

TABLE B-2 *(cont.)*

	All Institutions	Research & Doctorate-Granting	Comprehensive	Liberal Arts	Two-Year
In fraternity/sorority housing					
Less than 1 percent	75%	15%	67%	65%	98%
1-9 percent	13	54	22	8	2
10 percent or more	12	31	11	28	0
Leave during or after first year					
Less than 1 percent	1	2	3	2	0
1-9 percent	10	12	6	23	5
10-24 percent	41	57	63	49	21
25-49 percent	41	28	22	24	62
50 percent or more	7	2	6	2	12
Black					
Less than 5 percent	46	46	38	59	44
5-15 percent	39	53	47	37	35
More than 15 percent	15	1	16	4	21
Hispanic					
Less than 1 percent	15	6	11	15	19
1-9 percent	75	89	74	81	70
10 percent or more	10	5	15	4	11

TABLE B-2 (cont.)

	All Institutions	Research & Doctorate-Granting	Comprehensive	Liberal Arts	Two-Year
Asian American					
Less than 1 percent	18%	8%	15%	19%	22%
1-9 percent	79	77	83	79	77
10 percent or more	3	15	2	2	1
American Indian					
Less than 1 percent	42	49	45	58	32
1-9 percent	57	51	55	42	65
10 percent or more	1	0	0	0	3

SOURCE: The American Council on Education and the National Association of Student Personnel Administrators, National Survey of Chief Student Affairs Officers, 1989.

TABLE B-3

Changes in Student Affairs Budget
(Percentage Giving Each Response)

	All Institutions	Research & Doctorate-Granting	Comprehensive	Liberal Arts	Two-Year
Budget changes over the past five years:					
Increases exceeding inflation	20%	27%	24%	32%	12%
Increases matching inflation	34	43	38	26	33
Little or no change	33	14	24	22	46
Budget cuts or reversions	13	16	14	20	9

SOURCE: The American Council on Education and the National Association of Student Personnel Administrators, National Survey of Chief Student Affairs Officers, 1989.

TABLE B-4

Rating of Quality of Campus Life
(Percentage Giving Each Response)

	All Institutions	Research & Doctorate-Granting	Comprehensive	Liberal Arts	Two-Year
Campus life today is:					
Excellent	12%	20%	16%	14%	7%
Good	69	65	66	73	69
Fair	19	14	17	12	23
Poor	1	1	1	1	1
Compared with five years ago:					
Better	58	69	69	73	45
Largely the same	32	23	23	21	43
Not as good	10	8	8	7	12

SOURCE: The American Council on Education and the National Association of Student Personnel Administrators, National Survey of Chief Student Affairs Officers, 1989.

TABLE B-5

Five-Year Change in Problems of Campus Life
(Percentage Giving Each Response)

	All Institutions	Research & Doctorate-Granting	Comprehensive	Liberal Arts	Two-Year
Inadequate facilities for campus gatherings					
Greater problem	42%	37%	41%	48%	40%
About the same	30	36	29	26	32
Less of a problem	11	15	12	13	8
Not a problem	17	13	19	13	19
Inadequate facilities for commuter students					
Greater problem	36	29	31	40	37
About the same	32	45	38	40	23
Less of a problem	10	9	11	9	11
Not a problem	22	17	19	12	29
Alcohol abuse					
Greater problem	32	50	39	40	22
About the same	41	34	50	36	40
Less of a problem	14	14	7	18	15
Not a problem	13	3	4	6	23

TABLE B-5 (cont.)

	All Institutions	Research & Doctorate-Granting	Comprehensive	Liberal Arts	Two-Year
Few students participate in campus events					
Greater problem	29%	11%	26%	27%	35%
About the same	47	60	45	41	48
Less of a problem	15	16	23	21	7
Not a problem	9	14	6	10	10
Inadequate services for commuter students					
Greater problem	28	24	26	38	24
About the same	36	49	41	35	32
Less of a problem	13	11	15	13	12
Not a problem	24	16	18	15	32
Drug/substance abuse					
Greater problem	25	21	33	17	25
About the same	45	56	51	52	37
Less of a problem	14	19	12	14	14
Not a problem	16	4	4	16	25

TABLE B-5 (cont.)

	All Institutions	Research & Doctorate-Granting	Comprehensive	Liberal Arts	Two-Year
Overcrowded or outdated residence halls					
Greater problem	25%	23%	32%	43%	9%
About the same	23	36	12	24	26
Less of a problem	14	24	24	17	3
Not a problem	38	17	32	15	62
Thefts					
Greater problem	22	33	27	25	17
About the same	56	56	56	58	55
Less of a problem	9	10	11	12	7
Not a problem	13	1	6	5	21
Violations of honor codes or rules of academic integrity					
Greater problem	19	22	17	29	14
About the same	49	74	57	53	40
Less of a problem	5	1	9	5	5
Not a problem	27	3	18	13	41

TABLE B-5 (cont.)

	All Institutions	Research & Doctorate-Granting	Comprehensive	Liberal Arts	Two-Year
Incidents involving physical violence					
Greater problem	18%	34%	24%	21%	12%
About the same	43	52	49	32	43
Less of a problem	9	11	12	16	3
Not a problem	30	3	14	31	42
Suicides and suicide attempts					
Greater problem	17	34	28	19	8
About the same	44	55	47	54	37
Less of a problem	9	4	9	11	8
Not a problem	30	7	16	16	47
Inadequate security					
Greater problem	17	14	17	26	14
About the same	35	50	29	26	40
Less of a problem	18	24	27	25	8
Not a problem	30	11	27	23	38

TABLE B-5 (cont.)

	All Institutions	Research & Doctorate-Granting	Comprehensive	Liberal Arts	Two-Year
Vandalism and destruction of property					
Greater problem	16%	20%	16%	17%	16%
About the same	45	53	49	39	44
Less of a problem	19	25	25	30	11
Not a problem	20	2	11	14	30
Excessive noise and disruptiveness in campus residences					
Greater problem	16	9	17	27	11
About the same	41	70	45	50	26
Less of a problem	19	17	27	19	15
Not a problem	24	4	12	4	48
Racial tensions/hostilities					
Greater problem	16	32	17	21	11
About the same	35	52	45	35	27
Less of a problem	15	11	11	16	18
Not a problem	34	6	27	28	44

TABLE B-5 (cont.)

	All Institutions	Research & Doctorate-Granting	Comprehensive	Liberal Arts	Two-Year
Disruptive behavior by nonstudents					
Greater problem	16%	18%	19%	19%	14%
About the same	30	43	30	37	25
Less of a problem	8	13	13	9	5
Not a problem	45	26	37	36	57
Poor academic advising					
Greater problem	15	22	18	12	14
About the same	37	53	38	44	31
Less of a problem	28	20	31	28	27
Not a problem	20	5	14	15	27
Lack of civility when disputes arise					
Greater problem	15	23	17	25	8
About the same	36	55	43	36	30
Less of a problem	8	6	14	9	6
Not a problem	40	16	26	30	55

TABLE B-5 (cont.)

	All Institutions	Research & Doctorate-Granting	Comprehensive	Liberal Arts	Two-Year
Sexual harassment					
Greater problem	14%	32%	17%	11%	12%
About the same	50	62	57	59	42
Less of a problem	9	5	11	5	10
Not a problem	26	2	15	25	36
Racial intimidation/harassment					
Greater problem	11	24	11	13	8
About the same	35	57	43	38	27
Less of a problem	13	13	12	15	13
Not a problem	40	7	34	34	52
Crude and offensive behavior at sports events					
Greater problem	11	13	11	14	9
About the same	26	49	29	33	18
Less of a problem	17	19	20	19	14
Not a problem	46	19	40	34	59

TABLE B-5 (cont.)

	All Institutions	Research & Doctorate-Granting	Comprehensive	Liberal Arts	Two-Year
Rape/sexual assault					
Greater problem	10%	23%	15%	15%	4%
About the same	40	67	53	54	22
Less of a problem	10	6	12	8	11
Not a problem	40	3	20	23	63
Incidents involving guns and other weapons					
Greater problem	8	7	17	7	5
About the same	26	52	28	29	19
Less of a problem	16	13	23	9	17
Not a problem	50	28	32	55	59
Greek life problems					
Greater problem	8	28	12	10	0
About the same	21	41	34	23	5
Less of a problem	10	25	15	11	3
Not a problem	61	6	39	55	91

TABLE B-5 (cont.)

	All Institutions	Research & Doctorate-Granting	Comprehensive	Liberal Arts	Two-Year
Excessive drinking at sports events					
Greater problem	5%	8%	6%	3%	4%
About the same	19	36	22	14	17
Less of a problem	17	31	23	24	9
Not a problem	59	26	50	59	70
Disruptive behavior at commencement or convocation ceremonies					
Greater problem	3	9	3	6	1
About the same	19	25	20	23	16
Less of a problem	14	33	13	11	12
Not a problem	64	33	63	60	71
Hazing incidents					
Greater problem	3	10	4	5	0
About the same	18	38	29	22	6
Less of a problem	21	37	35	32	5
Not a problem	58	15	33	42	89

TABLE B-5 (cont.)

	All Institutions	Research & Doctorate-Granting	Comprehensive	Liberal Arts	Two-Year
Disruptive protest demonstrations					
Greater problem	1%	10%	1%	1%	0%
About the same	13	22	13	19	9
Less of a problem	15	26	24	14	8
Not a problem	71	42	61	66	83
Other					
Greater problem	63	37	69	0	0
About the same	37	63	31	0	0
Less of a problem	0	0	0	0	0
Not a problem	0	0	0	0	0

SOURCE: The American Council on Education and the National Association of Student Personnel Administrators, National Survey of Chief Student Affairs Officers, 1989.

TABLE B-6

Five-Year Change in Campus Crime
(Percentage Giving Each Response)

	All Institutions	Research & Doctorate-Granting	Comprehensive	Liberal Arts	Two-Year
Number of reported crimes on campus					
Increase	26%	43%	35%	32%	16%
No change	50	31	40	45	59
Decrease	15	21	16	12	15
Don't know	9	4	9	11	10
Severity of crimes on campus					
Increase	14	20	16	14	11
No change	63	60	60	61	65
Decrease	16	16	19	21	13
Don't know	7	4	5	3	1
Number of reported crimes in surrounding community					
Increase	50	59	54	42	49
No change	28	19	23	30	32
Decrease	3	4	4	5	1
Don't know	19	18	19	23	17

TABLE B-6 *(cont.)*

	All Institutions	Research & Doctorate-Granting	Comprehensive	Liberal Arts	Two-Year
Severity of crimes in surrounding community					
Increase	41%	56%	46%	30%	41%
No change	39	23	32	46	43
Decrease	3	3	4	4	3
Don't know	17	19	18	20	14

SOURCE: The American Council on Education and the National Association of Student Personnel Administrators, National Survey of Chief Student Affairs Officers, 1989.

TABLE B-7

Five-Year Change in Violation of Institutional Rules
(Percentage Giving Each Response)

	All Institutions	Research & Doctorate-Granting	Comprehensive	Liberal Arts	Two-Year
Campus residence halls:					
Number of violations					
Increase	26%	31%	27%	32%	18%
No change	52	59	43	43	67
Decrease	19	10	29	24	10
Don't know	2	0	1	1	5
Severity of violations					
Increase	12	15	13	16	5
No change	67	74	65	61	73
Decrease	20	11	21	22	22
Don't know	1	0	1	1	0
Fraternity/sorority system:					
Number of violations					
Increase	17	42	13	18	5
No change	58	42	59	49	76
Decrease	18	16	19	25	9
Don't know	7	0	9	8	10

TABLE B-7 (cont.)

	All Institutions	Research & Doctorate-Granting	Comprehensive	Liberal Arts	Two-Year
Severity of violations					
Increase	10%	20%	9%	10%	5%
No change	65	66	66	47	80
Decrease	18	14	17	33	10
Don't know	7	0	8	10	5
Other campus settings:					
Number of violations					
Increase	13	16	17	12	11
No change	67	72	59	63	73
Decrease	14	6	19	18	11
Don't know	6	5	5	7	5
Severity of violations					
Increase	10	13	14	11	7
No change	68	75	66	62	71
Decrease	14	8	13	16	16
Don't know	7	3	8	11	6

SOURCE: The American Council on Education and the National Association of Student Personnel Administrators, National Survey of Chief Student Affairs Officers, 1989.

TABLE B-8

Racial/Ethnic Incidents and Regulation of Student Conduct

(Percentage Giving Each Response)

	All Institutions	Research & Doctorate-Granting	Comprehensive	Liberal Arts	Two-Year
Racial/ethnic incidents this year					
None	78%	50%	73%	76%	87%
One	12	26	16	14	6
More than one	10	24	11	9	7
Five-year change in racial/ethnic incidents					
Increase	15	30	15	18	12
No change	73	61	76	69	74
Decrease	12	9	9	12	14
Five-year change in regulation of student conduct					
More explicit	54	63	55	66	48
About the same	45	37	45	31	52
Less explicit	1	0	0	3	0
More systematic enforcement	54	61	65	68	40
About the same	44	38	34	27	59
Less systematic enforcement	2	1	1	5	1

TABLE B-8 (cont.)

	All Institutions	Research & Doctorate-Granting	Comprehensive	Liberal Arts	Two-Year
Campus has written policy on bigotry, racial harassment or intimidation					
Yes	60%	69%	61%	58%	59%
Is developing one	11	18	15	14	7
No	29	13	24	28	34

SOURCE: The American Council on Education and the National Association of Student Personnel Administrators, National Survey of Chief Student Affairs Officers, 1989.

TABLE B-9

Changes in Student Orientation Programs
(Percentage Giving Each Response)

	All Institutions	Research & Doctorate-Granting	Comprehensive	Liberal Arts	Two-Year
Program changes over the last five years:					
More time spent in orientation	59%	58%	62%	58%	58%
About the same	35	40	34	31	36
Less now	6	2	4	11	6
Broader coverage of issues	79	86	78	84	76
About the same	19	12	21	14	21
Narrower coverage of issues	3	2	1	2	4

SOURCE: The American Council on Education and the National Association of Student Personnel Administrators, National Survey of Chief Student Affairs Officers, 1989.

TABLE B-10

Five-Year Change in Concern About Campus Life
(Percentage Giving Each Response)

	All Institutions	Research & Doctorate-Granting	Comprehensive	Liberal Arts	Two-Year
Concerns expressed by:					
Parents					
Increased concern	45%	64%	66%	54%	26%
No change	47	30	31	39	61
Decreased concern	3	2	0	2	5
Don't know	6	3	2	4	9
Community representatives					
Increased concern	41	42	58	28	39
No change	47	51	32	46	54
Decreased concern	3	2	3	4	3
Don't know	9	4	8	21	5
Legislators					
Increased concern	33	43	37	20	36
No change	48	44	46	46	50
Decreased concern	2	3	1	0	4
Don't know	16	9	16	34	10

TABLE B-10 *(cont.)*

	All Institutions	Research & Doctorate-Granting	Comprehensive	Liberal Arts	Two-Year
Alumni/ae					
Increased concern	25%	39%	40%	32%	11%
No change	62	52	51	53	74
Decreased concern	3	2	1	4	3
Don't know	11	7	7	11	13
Donors					
Increased concern	22	32	27	35	11
No change	56	54	52	34	70
Decreased concern	1	3	1	0	1
Don't know	20	11	20	30	18

SOURCE: The American Council on Education and the National Association of Student Personnel Administrators, National Survey of Chief Student Affairs Officers, 1989.

TABLE B-11

Views on Improving Campus Life
(*Percentage Giving Each Response*)

	All Institutions	Research & Doctorate-Granting	Comprehensive	Liberal Arts	Two-Year
Greater effort to build a stronger overall sense of community					
Very important	77%	81%	74%	92%	72%
Somewhat important	21	18	23	8	27
Not important	1	0	3	1	1
Don't know	0	1	0	0	0
More interaction between students and faculty					
Very important	75	82	74	76	74
Somewhat important	23	16	25	23	22
Not important	2	1	1	0	4
Don't know	0	0	0	0	0
Expanded services for nontraditional students					
Very important	68	66	61	61	76
Somewhat important	27	29	33	38	19
Not important	4	4	6	1	5
Don't know	0	0	0	0	0

TABLE B-11 (cont.)

	All Institutions	Research & Doctorate-Granting	Comprehensive	Liberal Arts	Two-Year
More events that affirm the institution's mission, objectives and values					
Very important	67%	57%	72%	73%	63%
Somewhat important	30	40	24	24	33
Not important	3	3	3	3	4
Don't know	0	1	0	0	0
Closer links between classroom and out-of-class activities					
Very important	66	69	67	71	64
Somewhat important	27	28	29	27	25
Not important	7	3	2	3	11
Don't know	0	0	1	0	0
More collaborative learning among students					
Very important	61	49	64	59	63
Somewhat important	34	44	28	34	36
Not important	4	6	9	5	1
Don't know	1	1	0	2	0

TABLE B-11 (cont.)

	All Institutions	Research & Doctorate-Granting	Comprehensive	Liberal Arts	Two-Year
More leadership opportunities for students					
Very important	60%	89%	66%	62%	52%
Somewhat important	32	11	26	34	37
Not important	7	0	6	2	11
Don't know	1	0	1	2	0
Greater incentives for alcohol-free events					
Very important	59	63	61	62	56
Somewhat important	34	33	37	32	34
Not important	6	4	2	6	9
Don't know	1	0	0	0	1
More events that bring large numbers of students, faculty and staff together					
Very important	57	41	57	62	58
Somewhat important	36	51	38	30	35
Not important	7	7	4	8	7
Don't know	0	1	0	0	0

TABLE B-11 (cont.)

	All Institutions	Research & Doctorate-Granting	Comprehensive	Liberal Arts	Two-Year
More aggressive programs to prevent alcohol and drug abuse					
Very important	54%	41%	47%	44%	64%
Somewhat important	36	45	45	42	27
Not important	10	14	8	12	9
Don't know	0	0	0	1	0
Workshops on conflict resolution					
Very important	49	50	56	55	43
Somewhat important	35	39	36	31	35
Not important	15	11	8	13	19
Don't know	1	0	0	2	2
More explicit expectations for student behavior and responsibilities					
Very important	44	41	50	53	37
Somewhat important	46	49	43	36	51
Not important	10	10	6	9	12
Don't know	1	0	0	3	0

TABLE B-11 *(cont.)*

	All Institutions	Research & Doctorate-Granting	Comprehensive	Liberal Arts	Two-Year
Better orientation programs					
Very important	38%	45%	38%	35%	39%
Somewhat important	52	45	50	55	52
Not important	8	7	7	4	9
Don't know	2	3	5	5	0
Better campus communications					
Very important	37	38	40	38	35
Somewhat important	47	57	47	49	44
Not important	15	6	12	10	20
Don't know	1	0	1	3	0
New or revised statements on civility and respect for others					
Very important	33	38	39	37	28
Somewhat important	46	50	46	46	45
Not important	18	13	14	13	23
Don't know	3	0	1	4	5

TABLE B-11 (cont.)

	All Institutions	Research & Doctorate-Granting	Comprehensive	Liberal Arts	Two-Year
Better enforcement of rules governing student behavior					
Very important	32%	28%	32%	30%	33%
Somewhat important	51	54	51	59	47
Not important	17	17	17	11	19
Don't know	1	0	0	0	1
Greater understanding and awareness of racial/ethnic diversity					
Very important	27	25	31	38	21
Somewhat important	53	58	56	53	52
Not important	19	17	12	8	27
Don't know	0	0	1	1	0
Strengthened campus police and security					
Very important	27	21	28	39	22
Somewhat important	46	54	47	42	45
Not important	26	23	24	17	31
Don't know	1	1	1	2	1

TABLE B-11 *(cont.)*

	All Institutions	Research & Doctorate-Granting	Comprehensive	Liberal Arts	Two-Year
Better procedures for handling complaints and grievances					
Very important	25%	30%	22%	30%	24%
Somewhat important	52	56	55	54	49
Not important	20	14	19	14	25
Don't know	2	0	4	3	1
Other					
Very important	100	100	100	100	100
Somewhat important	0	0	0	0	0
Not important	0	0	0	0	0
Don't know	0	0	0	0	0

SOURCE: The American Council on Education and the National Association of Student Personnel Administrators, National Survey of Chief Student Affairs Officers, 1989.

TABLE B-12

"One Change" Student Affairs Officers Say They Would Make to Improve Campus Life
(Percentage Listing Each Response)

	All Institutions	Research & Doctorate-Granting	Comprehensive	Liberal Arts	Two-Year
Build or improve residences, student union or other campus facilities	24%	16%	16%	21%	33%
Improve faculty/staff/student interaction	16	24	14	9	19
Increase funds for Student Affairs	12	3	15	15	9
Build sense of community for all	5	6	3	8	4
Build or improve recreation center	5	3	7	4	6
Improve student involvement	5	3	4	4	8
Improve ethics, values, standards, respect for authority	5	3	3	6	5
Reduce alcohol/drug consumption	4	7	7	5	2

TABLE B-12 *(cont.)*

	All Institutions	Research & Doctorate-Granting	Comprehensive	Liberal Arts	Two-Year
Improve relations/increase diversity/retention—racial, religious	4%	3%	10%	3%	2%
Required program (orientation/course) for freshmen; mentoring	2	9	3	0	2
Improve academic advising	2	2	5	2	0
Give Student Affairs greater voice	2	2	0	3	2
More support and interest by president	2	2	0	2	4
Build or improve athletic facilities	2	1	4	0	2
More focus on activities for older students and off-campus students	2	0	0	3	2
Stress concern for "whole student"	1	5	0	3	0

TABLE B-12 *(cont.)*

	All Institutions	Research & Doctorate-Granting	Comprehensive	Liberal Arts	Two-Year
Reduce effects of and change Greek system	1%	3%	2%	3%	0%
More student housing/assistance	1	2	2	2	0
Strengthen security	1	2	0	3	0
Improve faculty retention	1	0	0	3	0
More social activities	1	0	0	0	2
Less territoriality	0	2	0	0	0
Parking	0	2	0	0	0
Eliminate deferred maintenance in residence halls	0	2	0	0	0
More emphasis on teaching; less on research	0	2	0	0	0

TABLE B-12 (cont.)

	All Institutions	Research & Doctorate-Granting	Comprehensive	Liberal Arts	Two-Year
Fill out fewer questionnaires	0%	0%	2%	0%	0%
Increase campus population	0	0	2	0	0
Increase library hours	0	0	2	0	0
Stricter conduct code for faculty	0	0	0	1	0
Emphasis on student leadership	0	0	0	0	0
Increase night life off campus for students	0	0	0	0	0

NOTE: The open-ended question read: "If you could make one change at your institution to improve the quality of campus life, what change would you make?"

SOURCE: The American Council on Education and the National Association of Student Personnel Administrators, National Survey of Chief Student Affairs Officers, 1989.

APPENDIX C

Technical Notes

THE CARNEGIE FOUNDATION for the Advancement of Teaching and the American Council on Education jointly conducted the National Survey of College and University Presidents. The National Survey of Chief Student Affairs Officers was administered by the American Council on Education and the National Association of Student Personnel Administrators. Both of these surveys on the quality of campus life were completed in 1989.

The institutional population from which the study's sample was drawn is a modification of that found in The Carnegie Foundation for the Advancement of Teaching's *A Classification of Institutions of Higher Learning,* 1987 edition. This list of institutions was chosen because it provided a degree of differentiation for universities and for liberal arts colleges. Furthermore, the classification system proposed by the U.S. Department of Education in the early 1980s that paralleled to some degree the Carnegie system was never updated.

The Carnegie list was matched with data from the most recent institutional data from the Department of Education, the 1987-88 Institutional Characteristics File. Institutions on the Carnegie file that did not appear on the Department of Education's file were traced to learn if they had changed their name, merged with other institutions, changed accreditation status, or closed.

It was assumed that the primary thrust of the survey was to look at life on campus as it is experienced by most undergraduate students. It was therefore decided to eliminate graduate-only institutions, specialized institutions (such as schools of religion and theology, medicine, law, teacher education, engineering and technology, business and management, art, music and design), and institutions of less than 300 enrollment as reported on the Department of Education's 1987-88 computer tape of institutional characteristics.

137

These procedures netted a population of 2,540 institutions. From this total, 19 institutions were eliminated because they were to participate in the site visit portion of the survey. Their willingness to undergo the close scrutiny of the visitors was deemed to be a sufficient contribution to the study. Two additional institutions were found to have been closed. Thus, the survey's population consists of a total of 2,519 colleges and universities with undergraduate programs and with total enrollments of 300 or more students.

For sampling purposes, it was decided to adjust the Carnegie classification categories somewhat. Consequently, the four categories of major universities (Research Universities I and II, and Doctorate-granting Universities and Colleges I and II) were consolidated into two strata, research universities and doctorate-granting universities. The two categories of Comprehensive Universities and Colleges were combined into one. However, the two liberal arts college categories remain separate, and all the two-year institutions remained in a single stratum.

Responses were received from 382 institutions in the National Survey of College and University Presidents (including 105 research and doctorate-granting institutions, 76 comprehensive institutions, 112 liberal arts institutions and 89 two-year colleges) representing a 76 percent response rate. In the National Survey of Chief Student Affairs Officers, 355 institutions responded (including 95 research and doctorate-granting institutions, 82 comprehensive institutions, 102 liberal arts institutions, and 76 two-year colleges), resulting in a 71 percent response rate. All data is weighted. *Some figures in the tables may not add up to 100 percent due to rounding.*

A few questions on the survey instruments were constructed to elicit an open-ended response. For example, presidents were asked, "During 1988-89, what three campus-life issues on your campus have given you the greatest concern?" The responses to these questions were grouped and coded by the survey administrators.

A third survey, The Carnegie Foundation for the Advancement of Teaching's 1989 National Survey of Faculty, is mentioned periodically. This questionnaire was mailed to 10,000 faculty at two-year and four-year institutions. Responses were received from 5,450.

Carnegie Classifications

THE 1987 CARNEGIE CLASSIFICATION includes all colleges and universities in the United States listed in the 1985-86 *Higher Education General Information Survey of Institutional Characteristics*. It groups institutions into categories on the basis of the level of degree offered—ranging from prebaccalaureate to the doctorate— and the comprehensiveness of their missions. The categories are as follows:

Research Universities I: These institutions offer a full range of baccalaureate programs, are committed to graduate education through the doctorate degree, and give high priority to research. They receive annually at least $33.5 million in federal support and awarded at least 50 Ph.D. degrees each year.

Research Universities II: These institutions offer a full range of baccalaureate programs, are committed to graduate education through the doctorate degree, and give high priority to research. They receive annually at least $12.5 million in federal support and awarded at least 50 Ph.D. degrees each year.

Doctorate-granting Universities I: In addition to offering a full range of baccalaureate programs, the mission of these institutions includes a commitment to graduate education through the doctorate degree. They award at least 40 Ph.D. degrees annually in five or more academic disciplines.

Doctorate-granting Universities II: In addition to offering a full range of baccalaureate programs, the mission of these institutions includes a commitment to graduate education through the doctorate degree. They award annually 20 or more Ph.D. degrees in at least one discipline or 10 or more Ph.D. degrees in three or more disciplines.

Comprehensive Universities and Colleges I: These institutions offer baccalaureate programs and, with few exceptions, graduate education through the master's degree. More than half of their baccalaureate degrees are awarded in two or more occupational or professional disciplines such as engineering or business administration. All of the institutions in this group enroll at least 2,500 students.

Comprehensive Universities and Colleges II: These institutions award more than half of their baccalaureate degrees in two or more occupational or professional disciplines, such as engineering or business administration, and many also offer graduate education through the master's degree. All of the institutions in this group enroll between 1,500 and 2,500 students.

Liberal Arts Colleges I: These highly selective institutions are primarily undergraduate colleges that award more than half of their baccalaureate degrees in art and science fields.

Liberal Arts Colleges II: These institutions are primarily undergraduate colleges that are less selective and award more than half of their degrees in liberal arts fields. This category also includes a group of colleges that award less than half of their degrees in liberal arts fields but, with fewer than 1,500 students, are too small to be considered comprehensive.

Two-Year Community, Junior, and Technical Colleges: These institutions offer certificate or degree programs through the Associate of Arts level and, with few exceptions, offer no baccalaureate degrees.

140

NOTES

PROLOGUE *Search for Renewal*

1. Helen Lefkowitz Horowitz, *Campus Life* (New York: Alfred A. Knopf, 1987), p. 68.

2. Calculated from U.S. Bureau of Census, *Historical Statistics of the United States, Colonial Times to 1970, Bicentennial Edition, Part 1* (Washington, D.C.: 1975), pp. 382-85. Also Victor J. Baldridge, et al., *Policy Making and Effective Leadership* (San Francisco: Jossey-Bass, 1978), p. 253.

3. David F. Allmandinger, Jr., "New England Students and the Revolution in Higher Education, 1800-1900," in *The Social History of American Higher Education,* ed. B. Edward McClellan and William J. Reese (Urbana and Chicago: University of Illinois Press, 1988), p. 67.

CHAPTER 1 *A Purposeful Community*

1. American Council on Education, "More College Students Combine Work and Study," news release, Washington, D.C., 4 Sept. 1989.

2. Alexander W. Astin, Follow-up Trends for 1985-1988, Four Years After Entry. Unpublished information provided to the Carnegie Foundation for the Advancement of Teaching.

3. The Carnegie Foundation for the Advancement of Teaching, National Survey of Undergraduates, 1984.

4. The Carnegie Foundation for the Advancement of Teaching, *The Condition of the Professoriate: Attitudes and Trends, 1989* (Princeton, NJ: Carnegie Foundation for the Advancement of Teaching, 1989), pp. 19, 21-22.

5. Parker Palmer, *To Know As We Are Known* (New York: Harper & Row, 1983).

CHAPTER 2   *An Open Community*

1. The Carnegie Foundation for the Advancement of Teaching and the American Council on Education, National Survey of College and University Presidents, 1989.

2. The American Council on Education and the National Association of Student Personnel Administrators, National Survey of Chief Student Affairs Officers, 1989.

3. John Doe v. University of Michigan, *No. 89-71683, U.S. District Court, Eastern Division of Michigan, Southern Division, 1989.*

4. The 1975 Report of the Committee on Freedom of Expression at Yale, chaired by Professor C. Vann Woodward, pp. 10-12.

5. Steven B. Sample, "Viewpoint of the President," *The Spectrum* (State University of New York at Buffalo), 4 Dec. 1989, p.11.

6. Derek C. Bok, "Reflections on Free Speech: An Open Letter to the Harvard Community," *Educational Record,* Winter 1985, pp. 4-8.

7. Ibid.

142

8. Wayne Booth, "Mere Rhetoric, and the Search for Common Learning," *Common Learning* (Washington, D.C.: Carnegie Foundation for the Advancement of Teaching, 1981), p. 54.

9. Steven B. Sample, ibid.

CHAPTER 3   *A Just Community*

1. American Council on Education, "Minorities in Higher Education," Sixth Annual Status Report, Washington, D.C., 1987, p. 3.

2. David Maraniss, "Hard Choices in Black and White," *The Washington Post,* 7 March 1990, p. A16.

3. The Carnegie Foundation for the Advancement of Teaching and the American Council on Education, National Survey of College and University Presidents, 1989.

4. Edward B. Fiske, "The Undergraduate Hispanic Experience: A Case of Juggling Two Cultures," *Change,* May/June 1988, p. 31.

5. Ibid., p. 32.

6. "Final Report on Recent Incidents at Ujama House," *Stanford Daily,* 18 Jan. 1989, pp. 7-10.

7. Courtney Leatherman, "More Anti-Semitism Is Being Reported on Campuses, but Educators Disagree on How to Respond to It," *Chronicle of Higher Education,* 7 Feb. 1990, p. 1.

8. Quoted in Martha Minow, "On Neutrality, Equality, and Tolerance: New Norms for a Decade of Distinction," *Change,* Jan./Feb. 1990, pp. 19-20.

9. Nannerl Keohane, "Response from the President to the Report of the Task Force on Racism: Progress Report and Working Plan," Wellesley College, 24 Oct. 1989.

10. Adrienne Rich, *On Lies, Secrets and Silence: Selected Prose 1966-1978* (New York: W. W. Norton & Co., Inc. 1980).

11. Carol S. Pearson, Donna L. Shavlik, and Judith G. Touchton, eds., *Educating the Majority: Women Challenge Tradition in Higher Education* (New York: American Council on Education/Macmillan, 1989), pp. 32-45.

12. Edward B. Fiske, citing the work of Catherine G. Krupnics, "Lessons," *The New York Times,* 11 April 1990, p. B8.

13. Mary M. Leonard and Brenda Alpert Sigall, "Empowering Women Student Leaders: A Leadership Development Model," in Carol S. Pearson, et al., eds., *Educating the Majority: Women Challenge Tradition in Higher Education* (New York: American Council on Education/Macmillan, 1989), p. 231.

14. Roberta M. Hall and Bernice R. Sandler, *Out of the Classroom: A Chilly Campus Climate for Women?* A publication of the Project on the States and Education of Women, Association of American Colleges, Washington, D.C., October 1984.

15. SHARE office (Sexual Harassment/Assault Advising, Resources, and Education), Princeton University, "What You Should Know About Sexual Harassment," brochure. Credit to Harvard University, "Tell Someone," brochure, and the University of Massachusetts at Amherst, "Sexual Harassment: the Problem, the Policy, the Procedure."

16. The Carnegie Foundation for the Advancement of Teaching, National Survey of Undergraduates, 1984.

17. Martha Minow, p.24.

18. *The Michigan Mandate: A Strategic Linking of Academic Excellence and Social Diversity,* a report from the University of Michigan, April 1989.

CHAPTER 4 *A Disciplined Community*

1. The Carnegie Foundation for the Advancement of Teaching and the American Council on Education, National Survey of College and University Presidents, 1989.

2. The Carnegie Foundation for the Advancement of Teaching, *The Condition of the Professoriate: Attitudes and Trends, 1989* (Princeton, NJ: Carnegie Foundation for the Advancement of Teaching, 1989), p. 36.

3. "Drug Use by Students Has Declined, Study Finds," *The Chronicle of Higher Education,* 21 Feb. 1990, P. A2.

4. The Carnegie Foundation for the Advancement of Teaching, National Survey of Undergraduates, 1984.

5. The American Council on Education and the National Association of Student Personnel Administrators, National Survey of Chief Student Affairs Officers, 1989.

6. "Students Still Drink, Fewer Drive Drunk," *Notes,* the newsletter of the Association of Governing Boards of Universities and Colleges, Washington, D.C., Feb./March 1989, p. 1.

7. The American Council on Education and the National Association of Student Personnel Administrators, National Survey of Chief Student Affairs Officers, 1989.

8. The Carnegie Foundation for the Advancement of Teaching, Campus Visits, 1989.

9. The Carnegie Foundation for the Advancement of Teaching and the American Council on Education, National Survey of College and University Presidents, 1989.

10. National Campus Violence Survey, General Report 1988. A report of the Center for the Study and Prevention of Campus Violence, Towson State University, Towson, Maryland, 1988.

11. The Carnegie Foundation for the Advancement of Teaching, National Survey of Undergraduates, 1984.

12. Kenneth R. R. Gros Louis, Chancellor, Speech to the Faculty Council of the Indiana University at Bloomington, 18 Oct. 1988.

13. The Carnegie Foundation for the Advancement of Teaching and the American Council on Education, National Survey of Chief Student Affairs Officers, 1989.

14. Margaret Platt Jendrek, "Faculty Reactions to Academic Dishonesty," *Journal of College Student Development,* Sept. 1989, vol. 30, p. 401.

15. The Carnegie Foundation for the Advancement of Teaching, *The Condition of the Professoriate: Attitudes and Trends, 1989* (Princeton, NJ: Carnegie Foundation for the Advancement of Teaching, 1989) p. 26.

16. Margaret Platt Jendrek, p. 402.

17. Ibid., p. 404.

1. Mary E. Clark, "Meaningful Social Bonding as a Universal Human Need," in *Conflict: Human Needs Theory,* ed. John W. Burton (New York: St. Martin's Press, in press, 1990).

2. The Carnegie Foundation for the Advancement of Teaching, National Survey of Undergraduates, 1984.

3. The Carnegie Foundation for the Advancement of Teaching and the American Council on Education, National Survey of College and University Presidents, 1989.

4. Ibid.

5. The Carnegie Foundation for the Advancement of Teaching, National Survey of Undergraduates, 1984.

6. Chuck V. Loring, "A Time for Action—A Message from the President," *National Interfraternity Conference Annual Report 1988,* Indianapolis, Indiana, 1988.

7. The Board of Directors, American Council on Education, news release, 4 Sept. 1989.

8. The Carnegie Foundation for the Advancement of Teaching and the American Council on Education, National Survey of College and University Presidents, 1989.

9. Ibid.

10. The American Council on Education and the National Association of Student Personnel Administrators, National Survey of Chief Student Affairs Officers, 1989.

CHAPTER 6 *A Celebrative Community*

1. The Carnegie Foundation for the Advancement of Teaching, Campus Visits, 1989.

2. We are indebted to George D. Kuh, John H. Schuh, and Elizabeth J. Whitt and Associates for permission to use these examples taken from a book to be published in 1991 by Jossey-Bass, tentatively titled *Involving Colleges: Encouraging Student Learning and Personal Development Through Out-of-Class Experiences.*

3. Ibid.

4. Ibid.

5. Woodrow Wilson, ''What Is a College For?'' in *The Papers of Woodrow Wilson,* vol. 19, ed. Arthur S. Link (Princeton: Princeton University Press, 1975), p. 344. (The article originally appeared in *Scribner's Magazine,* 46 [1909], pp. 570-77.)

EPILOGUE *Compact for Community*

1. Paul Goldberger, ''Why Design Can't Transform Cities,'' *The New York Times Magazine,* 25 June 1989, p. 1.

2. The Carnegie Foundation for the Advancement of Teaching and the American Council on Education, National Survey of College and University Presidents, 1989

INDEX

Academic departments, 13
Accreditation, 66–67
Affirmative action programs, 25–26
Alcohol abuse, 2, 35, 38–40, 49, 56;
    and campus crime, 42
Alumni, 58–59
American Council on Education, 2,
    26, 50
American Cultures (course of study),
    32
Anti-Semitism, 28
Athletics, 59–60

Beethoven, Ludwig von, 28
Behavior. *See* Conduct.
Bethany College, 15
Bill of Rights, 20
Blacks. *See* Minorities.
Bok, Derek, 22
Bonding, 47–54
Booth, Wayne, 23
Brooklyn College, 15

California, University of, 22; at
    Berkeley, 13, 32, 56
California State University, 52
Caring, 8, 47–54
Censorship, 19–23
Cheating, 45–46
Cherokee Nation, 60
City College, CUNY, 56
Civility, 7, 17–23; breakdown of, 2

Clark, Mary, 47
Codes of conduct, 5–6, 43–46
Colorado College, 34
Commitment, intellectual, 12, 14
Communication, 17, 23
Community colleges, 51, 53, 61
Conduct: codes of, 5, 6, 43–46; of
    students, 2, 37–46, 49
Counselling, 51–52; and sexual harass-
    ment, 34; and substance abuse, 40
Credentialism, 3, 63
Crime, 1, 2, 6, 40–44
CUNY. *See* City College.
Curriculum, 13, 14–16; and diversity,
    32

Discipline, 7, 37–46
Distribution requirements, 14–16
Diversity, 4, 7, 23, 25–35
Divisiveness. *See* Separatism
Drug abuse, 2, 35, 38–39, 49, 56

Earlham College, 13, 59
Evergreen State College, 57
Excellence, 12; and athletic programs,
    59–60

Faculty: opinion of students, 10–11,
    46; and teaching, 12
Farrakhan, Louis, 18
Fraternities, 45, 48–49
Free expression, 2, 17–23

Goldberger, Paul, 63
Governance, 2, 5–7, 37–46
Gros Louis, Kenneth R.R., 44

Harvard University, 22, 33
Higher education, transformation of, 4–6
Hills, Dominguez, 52
Hispanics. *See* Minorities.
Homosexuality, 19
Honor Code, 45–46

Identity, personal, 48
In loco parentis, 1, 5, 8, 37
Indiana University, 14, 40, 58

Jews. *See* Minorities.
Justice, 7, 21, 25–35, 66

King, Martin Luther, Jr., 27, 60–61

Leadership, 33, 64–65, 67
Learning, commitment to, 14
Legislatures, state, 6, 18
Literacy, 10
Living-Learning Center, 13–14
Louisville, University of, 13, 53
Loyalty, institutional, 49

Mankiller, Wilma, 60
Massachusetts, University of, 26
Meredith, James, 26
Miami University, 57
Michigan, University of, 19, 38
Minnesota, University of, 32, 35
Minorities, 25–35, 60–61
Minow, Martha, 35
Mission: of colleges and universities, 7, 9–16
Mississippi, University of, 26
Montgomery County Community College, 53, 58

Mt. Holyoke College, 32

National Interfraternity Conference, 49
Northern Arizona University, 60

Ohio Wesleyan University, 13
Orientation programs, 6, 55–56, 66

Palmer, Parker, 12
Parents, 6; *in loco parentis*, 1, 5, 8, 37
Parks, Rosa, 26
Piedmont Virginia Community College, 53
Princeton University, 34, 58–59
Public spaces, 63–64

Racism, 1, 2, 26–29, 31–32
Rape, 34
Religion, 5
Research and publication, 5, 12
Residential life, 5, 13–14
Responsibilities of colleges and universities, 1, 5, 6, 37
Rich, Adrienne, 32
Richmond, University of, 35
Rights of students, 6
Rituals, 55–62
Rochester, University of, 43

Saint Anselm College, 15
Sample, Stephen B., 21, 23
Security, 42–45
Separatism, 3, 29–31
Service, 47, 54
Sexism, 33
Sexual harassment, 17, 33–35
Skills, basic, 10
Sororities, 48–49
South Africa, 18–19
Standards, clarification of, 7

Stanford University, 27–28
State University of New York
    (SUNY), 15; at Brockport, 34; at
    Buffalo, 21
Students: characteristics of, 3–4; for-
    eign, 61; minority, 25–35; nontradi-
    tional, 51, 61; rights of, 6; work
    habits of, 9–11; and campus crime,
    42–43; and cooperative learning,
    12–13; and personal identity, 48
SUNY. *See* State University of New
    York.
Support systems, 47–54; for minority
    students, 26

"Take Back the Night," 34
Teaching, 3, 5, 12
Tenure, 12
Traditions, importance of, 8, 55–62

Transformation of higher education,
    4–6
Tufts University, 19, 32

Values, 7, 20, 35, 49, 65–66
Vermont, University of, 13–14

Weber State College, 13
Wellesley College, 31–32
Wells, Herman B., 58
Williams, Patricia, 28
Wilson, Woodrow, 59
Women, 2, 32–35
Woodward, C. Vann, 21

Xavier University, 56–57

Yale University, 20–21